RESCUE IN ALBANIA

ONE HUNDRED PERCENT OF JEWS IN ALBANIA RESCUED FROM HOLOCAUST

Harvey Sarner

Brunswick Press
Cathedral City, California, 1997

A paperback booklet entitled "The Jews of Albania" was published in 1992 by the same author and publisher, and some information is repeated.

Library of Congress catalog card number 96-080323
Printed in the United States Of America
Hard bound – ISBN 1-888521-09-0
Paper bound – ISBN 1-888521-11-2

First Edition
1997

∞∞∞∞∞∞∞∞∞∞∞∞∞∞∞∞∞∞∞∞∞∞∞∞
Published by Brunswick Press
P.O. Box 2244 Cathedral City, CA 92235
Co-published by the Frosina Foundation
∞∞∞∞∞∞∞∞∞∞∞∞∞∞∞∞∞∞∞∞∞∞∞∞

ALBANIAN AMERICAN CIVIC LEAGUE

Throughout their long history Albanians have desired and promoted peace and cooperation among all peoples. They have welcomed foreign visitors to their shores in a spirit of friendship. And, when Jewish refugees found their way to Albania, often fleeing for their lives, the Albanian peolple gave them shelter and protection.

Under fascist rule in Albania, as in other occupied countries during World War II, the Nazi authorities maintained strict surveillance over the Jewish population, registering both natives and new arrivals, and then herding them into camps. In Albania, Jews were removed from Burresi and Vlora, because these towns were strategic transportation links, and while the Nazis tried to deport all Jews not of Albanian citizenship, the Albanian people helped them escape concentration camps by taking them into their homes, giving them food and shelter, and hiding them.

At first, individual Albanians saved Jews on their own initiative. Later, when it became more dangerous, the task was organized by National Liberation Councils in the towns and villages. There were cases where Jewish families, in great danger of discovery, were moved from family to family and village to village, from town to country and back again. Sometimes Jewish families traveled with false passports given to them by Albanians. Often Jews were disguised as Albanian peasants and covertly relocated. In the process, many Albanians were arrested and shot to death for their heroic activities.

The Albanian American Civic League was founded in January 1989 to express the concerns of 400,000 Albanian Americans about the national identity and well-being of seven million Albanians living side by side in their original Balkan homeland – – in Albania, Kosova, western Macedonia, southern Montenegro, southern Serbia (Presheva), and northern Greece (Chamria). As a Member of the House of Representatives from 1985 to 1989, and as chair-

man of the Albanian American Civic League since that time, I have repeatedly sounded the alarm about Slobodan Milosevic's brutal treatment of the Albanian people of Kosova and in other parts of the Balkans under his influence. During my many trips to Kosova, Macedonia, and Albania, I led delegations of congress-men, human rights activists, and journalists to expose the horrific conditions under which Albanians have been forced to live – – under communism in Albania for fifty years since the end of World War II and under hostile Slavic regimes in the former Yugoslavia since the death of Marshall Tito in 1974.

It was my first trip to Albania in June 1990 with Congressman Tom Lantos, himself a Hungarian Jew who survived the Holocaust, that the then Communist Party leader and Albanian President, Ramiz Alia, in order to curry favor with Lantos, handed us a file containing the unpublicized heroic deeds of Albanians in rescuing Jews during World War II. These documents led to the research that resulted in the corroboration by Yad Vashem in Israel that the Albanian people deserved special recognition as a nation for their unique and courageous actions, which saved all Jews who resided in Albania and all who fled the Nazis from other European coun-tries and made it to Albania.

Hon. Joseph J. DioGuardi
Albanian American Civic League
61 Central Ave.
Ossining, NY 10562
Telephone (914) 762-5530
June 1998

ONE HUNDRED FIFTH CONGRESS
CONGRESS OF THE UNITED STATES
COMMITTEE ON INTERNATIONAL RELATIONS
HOUSE OF REPRESENTATIVES
WASHINGTON, DC 20515

TELEPHONE: (202) 225-5021

Rescue in Albania – – written by Harvey Sarner, an American Jewish philanthropist – – relates the remarkable stories of how the people of Albania risked their lives to save foreign and Albanian Jews during the Holocaust.

The accounts of how Danes and Bulgarians took great risks to save their Jewish fellow citizens are well known through historical studies and popularized docudramas. The equally compelling story of the courage and humanity of many Albanians during the dark days of World War II, however, is one that is unfamiliar to most Americans, and virtually no scholarly research has been done on this topic.

But this is a story that deserves to be told and a story about which we need to learn a great deal more. Harvey Sarner has performed an important service in bringing together these stories of the sacrifice and humanity of the Albanian people in preserving the lives of Jews.

This book also depicts many instances in which Albanians demonstrated their commitment to justice and peace. Earlier in this decade, the people of Albania shook off the shackles of communism and embraced democracy. They, however, did not have experience in the ways of democracy and the workings of a free market economy, and Albania has faced serious political, economic and social turmoil in the post-Communist era.

Beyond the borders of Albania proper is a significant ethnic

V

Albanian population in the province of Kosova and in Macedonia. While these Albanians share the same language, culture, values and commitment to justice of their relatives who live within the boundaries of Albania, they have faced a far different situation in their own lands.

Albanians in Kosova have been denied the most fundamental of human rights. The autonomy, which they enjoyed earlier under the government of the former Yugoslavia, has been systematically restricted and destroyed under an increasingly nationalist Serbian regime over the past ten years. Albanians who seek to exercise their fundamental civil rights have been systematically arrested, beaten, and tortured, and more recently have been subjected to violent military action and ethnic cleansing by Serbian authorities.

Albanians in neighboring Macedonia have also faced discrimination. Attempts to open a university in Tetova with a curriculum taught in Albanian and attempts to raise an Albanian flag alongside the Macedonian flag in Gostivar were prevented by police action.

It is a tragic irony that the children and grandchildren of the Albanians who helped Jews in Albania to escape during World War II now face discrimination and violence in Kosova and Macedonia. It is important to understand the background of these Albanians, and it is for this reason we urge you to take the time to read *Rescue in Albania*. This is a compelling story, and one that all of us can benefit from reading. At the same time, we must commit ourselves to see that the children and grandchildren of the brave heroes whose story this volume tells do not become victims of the forces of evil and repression that in every age work to suppress human freedom.

Tom Lantos
Member of Congress
(California)

Benjamin A. Gilman
Member of Congress
(New York)

This book is
Dedicated to

The Memory of
Josef Jakoel

A 20th Century Moses
who took his people to the
Promise Land

Facts About Albania

Albania on the west and southwest borders on the Adriatic and Ionian seas and on the north and east by Yugoslavia and on the southeast by Greece. Albania is a country with rugged terrain and independent people. After more than four decades of isolation and Communist rule, Albania is moving in the direction of democracy, and a free-market system.

Albania is a mountainous country with a population of 3.3 million and has an abundance of natural resources. It is relatively rich in minerals, especially chrome, and has deposits of oil, natural gas, bitumen, copper, iron, nickel, and salt. Albania today remains the least economically developed country in Europe.

In 1468, Albania became part of the Ottoman Empire. During the years of Ottoman rule most Albanians converted to Islam, and a substantial number immigrated to other Mediterranean regions. Ethnic Albanians comprise 96 percent of the population. 70 % of the population is of Moslem origin, 20% Eastern Orthodox Christian, and 10% Roman Catholic. The majority of the people are nonreligious. Albania is the only country in Europe with a Moslem* majority. In 1967 all religious institutions were closed by the government.

Higher education is offered by universities, teacher training schools, and agricultural colleges. In addition there are 20 privately run schools, 10 of which are licensed by the government. Several are run by the Roman Catholic church. Illiteracy, has been virtually eliminated in the adult population.

There are approximately 800 hospitals and more than 3,000 outpatient clinics.

Major cities include Tirane, the capital, Durrës (Durazzo), Shkoder (Scutari), Elbasan, Vlore (Valona), and Korçe (Koritza). Other cities or villages of importance to the rescue were Berat, Kavaja and Kruja. The capital is the only city with a population greater than 125,000.

In 1912, in the First Balkan War, the Turks were driven out, and Albania declared its independence.

During World War I, Albania was neutral but it became a battleground for other countries. In 1925 power was seized by Ahmed Zogu, a tribal chief. In 1928 he proclaimed Albania a monarchy and named himself King Zog. In 1939 Italy invaded Albania, forcing the king into exile.

During the 1960s and '70s Albania broke with the other Communist countires. After a dispute with Chinese leaders in 1978, Albania was completely isolated. The chief of the Communist Party, Enver Hoxha, ruled Albania from 1944 until his death in 1985. His successor, Ramiz Alia, slowly began to introduce reforms. Multi-party elections were held in March, 1991, and a coalition government was installed. Bans on religion and foreign travel were ended, and a new democratic constitution was adopted.
*Turkey is considered Asia.

Contents

Contents   Page

xi

Contents

Chapter Ten

The Jews After the War
Under the Communists
Israel
The Atheistic State
Jewish Life Before and During the Atheistic Period
Burial
Rabbis
Circumcision
Synagogues
Marriage
Kosher
Holidays
Hebrew Language
Jewish Homes
Anti-Semitism
Trades and Professions
Assimilation and Conversion
Names
Money to Buy Land in Israel
Emigration From Albania Before 1991

Chapter Eleven

Righteous Gentile Program
Righteous Gentiles Visit Israel
Exodus 1991
1991 Emigration
Albania Today

Introduction

This book is not a comprehensive history of Albania or even a comprehensive history of the Jews of Albania. The primary objective in writing this book is to call attention to the wonderful response of the people of Albania when foreign and Albanian Jews sought shelter from the Holocaust. The delay in telling the story of the rescue is due to the isolationist dictatorship that ruled Albania from the end of the Second World War until the early 1990s.

Albania is the only country in occupied Europe where Jews were not victims of the Nazi killing machine.[1] To understand the rescue of the Jews it is necessary to understand the general history of the Jews in Albania and a general view of Albania's history. Hopefully readers will find this very generalized history as fascinating as did the author.

Before becoming involved with the Albanian "Righteous Gentiles"[2] my only knowledge of Albania was the note that, at one time, my passport was not usable in 4 countries, Albania being one of the four. I was to learn that Albania is the poorest country in Europe and the only one with a Moslem majority. Moslems constitute about 70% of Albania's population and they sheltered Jews no less than did the Christians.

I was also to learn the wonderful fact that Albania was the one occupied country that evaded the Nazi persecution of Jews and had the unique survival rate of 100%. It was the only occupied country to have a larger Jewish population after the Second World War than before.

An American Jew, Herman Bernstein, while serving as the American Ambassador to Albania in the 1930s called this the most non anti-Semitic community in the world.

A second reason for writing this book is to call attention to the heroic efforts of the late Josef Jakoel[3] and his daughter, Felicita, in arranging the emigration of nearly all Albanian Jews to Israel in 1991. Josef Jakoel lived long enough to see the exodus to Israel and spent his last months of life in Eretz Israel, the land of Israel. He truly was a second Moses leading his people to their promised land.

From 1967 through the end of 1990 Albania was an atheistic state and a closed society, so closed, that it was a crime to read foreign literature, and so atheistic that it was a crime to give a child a Biblical name. The changes away from the closed and atheistic society occurred at about the time the Albanian Jews emigrated to Israel.

Jakoel characterized the Albanian Jews as "Romaniots" descendants of an ancient Jewish culture. There is very little in the Jewish encyclopedia about Romaniots, much of which is wrong, according to Jakoel. The Romaniots have some unique customs, but there is no question that they are Jews.

The population figures for time and place are easily confused by the sources as well as by myself. The problem is that we are dealing with estimates, and they are often conflicting. All population figures should be understood as estimates, and it's more important to understand the events and deeds than to be concerned with exact numbers.

And finally, I admit to a great confusion about Albanian names, both personal and place names, and apologize in advance to anyone whose name appears in the wrong time and place or is misspelled. With the assistance of Albanian speaking friends I have attempted to keep these errors to a minimum, but....

Harvey Sarner
Palm Springs, California

2

Footnotes:

1. The Jewish family Ardet was killed by the Nazis but were arrested as the family of a partisan and not as Jews.
2. The term "Righteous Gentile" applies to persons determined to have risked their lives to shelter Jews during the Holocaust.
3. Josef Rafael Jakoel was born in Vlora, Albania, in 1922 and was educated at the Italian Technical Institute of Commerce and graduated from Tirana State University. For the last ten years of his career he was a lecturer on accounting in the Higher Institute of Agriculture in Tirana. Much that has been written is based on letters and conversations with Josef Jakoel.

Chapter One

Albania at War

On April 7, 1939, Albania was invaded by Italian military forces and a week later the entire country was occupied by Italian soldiers. The Italians arrived at the Albanian ports and met little resistance. The Italian King took the crown of Albania and incorporated Albania into the Italian Empire.

The invasion of Albania was not without risks to the Italians. The mountainous nature of the country and the possibility of the Albanian King Zog arming the populous presented the danger of long guerrilla warfare. This necessitated lightning action. In the first week in April, 1939, the combined air, sea, and land forces of the Italians were too much for the Albanians who were already preparing themselves for guerrilla warfare.

King Zog and most of the "royalty" fled first to Greece and then to England. He was unsuccessful in his attempt to create a government in Exile like those created by other governments of occupied countries.

Greece
For the Italians, Albania was the road to Greece and a rocky road it was. On October 28, 1940, the Italians occupying Albania crossed the Albanian-Greco border and attacked Greece. The Greeks defeated the Italians in just 10 days. By November 22, there wasn't a single Italian soldier in Greece.

On two occasions Mussolini came to Albania to conduct the campaign against the Greeks, but he had no more success than his generals.

The Greeks went on the offensive and captured one of the Italian Naval bases, and held the key point of Korça, in Albania, until the Germans entered the conflict in April, 1941. The German invasion caused the withdrawal of Greek forces from Albania.

Neither side was sure about the Albanian army. The Greeks were suspicious of the 3,000 armed Albanians fighting at their side against the Italians and didn't cooperate with them. The Albanian army became part of the Italian army, but these were unreliable troops because of their anti-Italian attitudes.

By 1942 there was a steady increase in Albanian guerrilla activity and by the end of the year the Italians were no longer in complete control of the country.

There is no denying that there were quisling types in Albania as there were every place else and there was a collaborationist Albania Fascist Party. The collaborators were only a handful, while the guerrillas numbered in the tens of thousands. Nothing was found that would indict the collaborators insofar as specific Jewish interests were concerned.

In Albania there were many people who admired German culture and education but had no use for or connection with Nazis, in fact they had a deep antipathy towards them. There were families who sent their children to Germany or Austria (prewar) for their education, but they had no connection with Nazi ideology or Nazis invaders.

There were 33 known families of Albanian Jews on the eve of the invasion. The greater part of the population (15 families) lived in Vlora. The remainder were scattered around the country.

There was also an unknown number of foreign Jews in Albania, mostly in transit. This later group changed in number from day to day but measured in the hundreds.

Jews were not eligible to become members of the Albanian Fascist Party and it's doubtful that any would have joined even if eligible. Jews were not eligible to serve in the Albanian army during these years. That made sense as the Albanian army was part of the Italian army which was allied with the German army.

Albanian Jews served in the guerrilla armies, mostly with the partisans. Pepe Biro Kantos served as a partisan and stayed in the Albanian army after the war and became one of the highest ranking army officers. Dario Zhak Artiti was a partisan, so were David Koen, Ruben Zhak, Josef Bivas, and others.

In August, 1943, the Allies were contemplating the invasion of Albania and and an analysis was prepared of the scene in Albania before and during the Italian occupation. The situation changed rapidly when Italy capitulated. The displaced Italian soldiers were divided, some joining the Germans and some joining the partisans. The invasion plans were canceled.

The Germans arrived in September, 1943, and replaced the Italian puppet government with a Regency of four men headed by Mehdi Frashëri, a former Prime Minister.

The Regency abided by an agreement with Nazi Germany that allowed the free movement of the German army across Albania. In return, the Germans were not to interfere with Albanian internal affairs. This phrase "internal affairs " was important when the Germans later asked the Regency to provide a list of the Jews in Albania.

The agreement did not deter Albanian guerrillas from harassing the Germans, sometimes with dire results. In July, 1943, Albanian partisans attacked a German convoy and killed 60 German soldiers. The Germans retaliated by destroying the nearest village and killing 107, including women and children. During the war Albania suffered 28,000 killed and 12,600 wounded.

In November, 1944, the National Liberation Army defeated the Germans and on November 17, Tirana was liberated. On November 28, the liberation of Albania was complete. When the Second World War ended, the Regency was replaced by Communist partisans who took credit for forcing the Germans out of the country.

Civil War
There were various political and social philosophies among the anti-fascists which clouded an already complex picture. Two essential points are that the guerrillas of all denominations far out numbered the collaborationists, and the outcome of the inter-denomination conflict was that the Communist partisans became the new political power. The periods of democracy, royalty, and occupation were over. The fascist puppet Regency government was replaced with a home grown dictatorship that was to last for nearly half a century.

There was a three sided civil war; The National Liberation Army, who were known as the partisans (Communist), the National Front, and the Royalists (Legality Party). The National Liberation Army prevailed.

While the Nationalists, Royalists, and Communists (partisans) were concentrating on fighting the Germans, the Communists were also preparing in advance for the postwar period. The Communists had the advantage of support from Tito and his appreciable partisan force in Yugoslavia.

The Communists decided to liquidate the Nationalists, and there was a civil war in southern Albania that lasted about a year. Things got more complicated when some of the Nationalists, perhaps motivated by the massacres and atrocities by the Communists, went over to the German side. After the Nationalist were defeated, the Communists started a civil war with the Royalists in the north, and in a few weeks eliminated them as a military or political force.

Chapter Two

The Immigration

The First Wave

Legend has it that 2,000 years ago, a ship heading for Rome with a cargo of Jewish slaves from Palestine was blown off course and landed on the coast of Albania. The Roman's made no attempt to capture the escaped slaves and assumed they would be killed by wild animals. Apparently, the Roman's decided that the economics of the situation favored ordering a new supply of Jewish slaves rather than attempting to capture the ones who escaped.

According to legend, the beasts didn't get the Jewish slaves. The native people of the area[1] were fighting the Roman's and helped the Jews. This supposedly occurred in Illyria, a country you won't find on any modern map. Illyria was an old name for Albania. If the name sounds familiar this could be attributed to Shakespeare who uses Illyria as the shipwreck site in two of his plays.

The Encyclopedia Judaica[2] doesn't mention the shipwreck legend, yet it defines the Romaniots as being the descendants of the "First Wave." Except for the legend there is no connection between "Rome" and "Romaniots." It begs the question whether the name is the result of the legend or the legend is the result of the name.

There is no knowledge of the number of Jews in the area during this early period, but there is conclusive evidence of a Jewish presence, according to the Jewish-Roman historian, Flavous Josephus. There were some villages in north Albania which had all Jewish populations in ancient times, and some that have Jewish names, e.g. Palasa-Palestine and Orikum-Jericho.

Archaeologists found remnants of a synagogue in Dardania, an ancient port in Illyria. They date the ruins between the first and second centuries, C. E.

In the 4th century Albania became a part of the Byzantine Empire. There was a feudal system that lasted until the Ottoman invasion in the 15th century.

The Second Wave - From Salonika and Spain
The Romaniot Jews came to Albania from Salonika (Greece) at the end of the 14th century augmented by a small group from Hungary.

The Universal Jewish Encyclopedia states that in the early middle ages Jews came to Albania from Salonika. The "early middle ages" was before the expulsion from Spain which means the Jews coming to Albania from Salonika were unrelated to the Spanish Inquisition. These are the Romaniots that Josef Jakoel said arrived in Albania from northern Greece. (See, Romaniots)

There is evidence of a Jewish presence in the port city of Durrës in the early middle ages. There are records for August, 1319, that tell of trading for salt with "a Jewish merchant from Durrës." There is also documentation that on March 24, 1281, the Venetian Nikolai Martini was trading with two Jews of Durrës, Leone and Caro Calis. Another document states that in August, 1366, a Jew from Durrës sold salt to a Raguzian.[3]

The most significant emigration from Spain occurred at the end of the 15th century during the time of the Spanish Inquisition. This is considered the Second Wave. A large number of Jews fleeing the Inquisition went east to the areas controlled by the Ottoman Empire.

At the time of the Spanish Inquisition the Turkish Sultan invited the Jews to live under Moslem rule. Perhaps the Sultan had some compassion for Jews expelled from Spain, as Moslems also suffered under the Inquisition.

9

The Jews coming from Spain, known as "Sephardic" Jews, brought with them the Ladino language, an altered form of Spanish which is still spoken by the Jews of Turkey.

The Sultan saw benefits to his Empire from the absorption of the Jews of Spain, who bought with them knowledge and culture as well as commercial experience. The Ottoman were impressed and welcomed the Sephardic Jews who were highly educated and sophisticated, and were treated better than the native Romaniot Jews.

The emigrants from Spain first settled in Vlora where they built a synagogue and cemetery. They branched out from Vlora to Berat and Elbasan where they stayed for 200 years. Vlora was the biggest city of Albania at that time with 4000 inhabitants, more than half of whom were Jews from Spain. In Berat, there were 25 Jewish families the majority of whom were involved in trade. At the end of the 16th century, the Jews left Vlora for reasons unknown only to return in the mid-19th century.

There were Jews in Albania when the Sephardic Jews arrived, who traced their origins to the ancient schools of Palestine. These Jews mingled with the recent arrivals from Spain, but there was friction between them arising from the Sephardic claims of cultural superiority.

In the city of Salonika, in northern Greece, the local Jews were absorbed by the Sephardic. In Janina, and some other small cities in Greater Albania, the Sephardic were either absorbed by the Romaniot Greek-speaking Jews or moved further east.

The Sephardim in Albania disappeared in time. Jakoel said, "we know they went, but don't know when or where. We really aren't sure when they arrived or when they left, but we are sure they were there." There is concrete evidence of a Jewish presence. In one Moslem village they say they were Jews at one time, and all the native inhabitants have Jewish names. Prominent Moslem families throughout Albania claim they were Jews at one time.

Jews living in Albania had many good years, but they weren't all good. For example, during the Turkish-Venetian war of 1685 the Jews had to flee Vlora and went to Berat.

From 1788, and up to 1822, there was a hard period in Albanian history when Jews suffered under the Ottoman Sultan, and tyrant, Ai Pasha. Most of the bad years were associated with independence movements when the revolutionaries, mostly Greek-Albanians, equated Jews with Moslems and accused them of being loyal to the Ottoman rulers.

The Third Wave - From Janina to Vlora
Comparatively little is known about the Jews during the 18th and first half of the 19th centuries, a period during which there were few Jews living in Albania. The Third Wave reestablished the Jewish presence in Albania.

The Third Wave were "Romaniots" who first arrived in Vlora in the 1850s. They came from Janina and Preveza, both now in Greece. In the 1850s Janina and Vlora were in the same district in the Greater Albania portion of the Ottoman Empire (until 1878) so there was free movement between the two cities. The colony was started with men who came without their families, but there were exceptions. The first doctor to serve the Jewish community in the Vlora area was Dr. Solomon Menahem Jomtov who brought his wife with him in 1850.

When the settlement grew and prospered the married men sent for their families and the unmarried men returned to Janina to seek brides. At that time Janina had the largest Romaniot community.

The majority of the Romaniots who emigrated to Albania during the second half of the 19th century settled in Vlora (Valona), a sea port in the south which gave them access to the Adriatic Sea. When the first Jews came to Vlora it was a small closed community and everyone knew everybody else.

One of the first to make the move from Janina to Vlora was Josef Jakoel's grandfather. In time the Jews spread out from Vlora with settlements in Delvina and Gjirokastra. For a time there were 150 Jews in a town south of Vlora.

The Jewish community on the island of Corfu was started by Jews from Venice in the 14th century, although there is evidence of Jews living on Corfu as early as the 9th century. They spoke the Venetian dialect of Italian and this limited their relation with other Jewish communities. In Vlora most Jews spoke Albanian and Greek.

By the end of the 19th century the ties between Janina and the Romaniot community in Albania were strong, but had weaken from what they had been. At the same time the ties between the Albanian Romaniots and the island of Corfu became stronger. One has only to look at a map to see the reason. Corfu is so near and Janina is so far away.

The Jews of Albania maintained contact with the Jews of Janina and Corfu until the Second World War. Most of them had relatives in these two places and relied on the Jews of Janina and Corfu to periodically supply them with visits by a rabbi, a cantor, and a moel (the later is the person who does ritual circumcisions). Sadly, the Jewish community of Corfu disappeared during the Holocaust and only a few Jewish families survived in Janina.

The Third Wave was the last, although in 1894 a delegation of Russian Jews visited Albania to talk about settling there.(4) The Albanian Government indicated no objection if they weren't destitute and recommended that they settle on the coast "since the interior still contains some warlike races who are not friendly to foreigners." Thirty to forty Jewish families were expected. Nothing was found to indicate they arrived in Albania. They would have constituted the Fourth Wave.

There was another suggestion of a new wave of Jews coming to Albania, although as a practical matter this was

never a real possibility. King Zog, in exile in Great Britain during the Second World War, proposed to the British-Jewish leadership a plan for settling 50,000 Jewish families in his country. He described Albania as a rich country with poor people and said that the population of one million was in a country that could easily absorb a population of five million. He proposed that each of the 50,000 families be given a small farm from lands owned by the state.

The British Board of Deputies, the organization representing British Jews, took this proposal seriously enough to contact the British Foreign Office to see what they thought. The Foreign Office didn't take this proposal seriously, and doubted that King Zog would be able to reestablish the monarchy in Albania after the Second World War. Nothing ever came of this offer and King Zog died in exile.[5]

The Romaniots
According to the Encyclopedia Judaica, the term "Romaniot" refers to the original Jews of the Byzantine Empire. The Encyclopedia refers to Romaniots in only Janina, Kastor, and Chalcis, all in Greece, and ignores the Albanian Romaniots, who were the largest group in Europe until they emigrated to Israel in 1991.

The Romaniots are neither Askenaze (Yiddish speaking) nor Sephardic (Ladino speaking). The Jews of Albania are "Romaniot Greek Speaking Jews," although in recent years they would be better described as Albanian speaking. Jakoel commented that many of the Jews who came to Israel don't know they are Romaniots because of the lack of Jewish education in the past decades. Many have little knowledge of Jewish history or of their own backgrounds.

The Romaniots insist that they are not descendants of the Sephardic Jews who came from Spain. They claim to be descendants of Jews who lived in northern Greece since the destruction of the Second Temple in the first century. The

13

Encyclopedia Judaica[6] describe the Romaniots as being the descendants of the "First Wave." The Romaniots are proud of their ancient history.

For a short period there was a joining together of the Sephardic and Romaniot Jews, but they separated probably due to the fact that the Romaniots were more strict in following their religious rules. The Jews from Spain called the Romaniots "Grego," which in Spanish could mean a Greek, but it was also used as a pejorative against a Romaniot Jew. Each group was sincerely confident of its superiority over the other.

Vlora

The arrival of the Romaniots was not the first time there was an identifiable Jewish community in Vlora. In 1507 there were 97 Jewish households in Vlora, which increased to 609 households in 1520; most were refugees from Spain during the "Second Wave." Jews of Vlora were killed during the revolts against the Ottoman in the 16th century. The remaining Jews fled from the coast to the mountainous town of Berat during the Turkish-Venician war in the 17th century.

The city of Vlora has always been an important port and at times it had a large Jewish population. Old people tell of a synagogue in operation until 1915 which the Italians used as an armory, but we could find no trace of the synagogue. The legend is that the Italians, who occupied parts of Albania during the First World War, burned the synagogue and other buildings to widen the street so their artillery could pass.

We were too late to find the Jewish cemetery of Vlora. It had been destroyed and a private residence is to be built on the site. We did a little digging on the vacant construction site and found evidence that this had been a Jewish cemetery. We found a tombstone, chiseled on it was a Star of David, a name, Saba Matitia, and date of death, December 5, 1901.

14

There is currently no organized Jewish life in Vlora and Mr. J. Matattia's home is used as the gathering place for the holidays. There were only 60 Jews in Vlora, in 1990. According to Mr. Matattia, there was a large Jewish population about a hundred years ago that is said to have left Vlora overnight. Mr. J. Matattia's father, Mateo Matattia, was probably the most prominent Jew in Vlora, a member of the city council and a merchant.

The first modern Jewish settlement was in Vlora but the center of Jewish life later moved to Tirana, the capitol and largest city. Jakoel made the move in 1950, as did many others looking for opportunities, including the chance to attend Albania's university.

It's symbolic that when the first flag of Albanian independence was raised on November 28, 1912, it was in Vlora.

Footnotes:
1. Albanians consider themselves descendants of the Ilyrian people who settled here in 1200 B.C.E. The roots of the language are Indo-European.
2. Vol. 14, p.231.
3. A native of Sicily.
4. Jewish Chronicle, March 9, 1894, p.9.
5. UK PRO FO 371/37138.
6. Vol. 14, p.231.

Chapter Three

Ambassador Herman Bernstein
and the False Messiah

In the 1930s the American Ambassador to Albania was a Jew, Herman Bernstein. Ambassador Bernstein took an interest in Jewish history and did some exploring to find traces of early Jewish life in Albania. He was especially interested in finding information about Sabbatai Zvi, the False Messiah. He knew that old records indicate Zvi had been in the town of Ulqin, but he was not able to find Zvi's tomb or traces of Jewish life in that town.

But Ambassador Bernstein did find evidence of a large Jewish community in Albania in the 15th and 16th centuries. He quotes from a German document published in 1611, "...many of these places are inhabited by Jews who had gone to Albania from Ancona (Italy) during the period of Pope Paul IV, who intensified the inquisition."

Ambassador Bernstein wrote that the Patriarch of the Albanian Orthodox Church told him that in a section of Elbasan known even today as the Jewish Quarter, a Star of David can be seen on the upper part of a building. The concrete Star was subsequently removed from the building and the pieces can now be seen in the small museum in Elbasan.

The Ambassador conducted his own research in the Elbasan archives and found a record of a Turkish judge (1730s) trying Jewish merchants for violating Turkish law.[1]

Bernstein prophesied that Albania may soon again offer asylum to the new Jewish wanderers who find closed doors elsewhere.[2] This prediction was made in 1936.[3]

The False Messiah.

In the middle of the 17th century a soothsayer born in Ismir, Turkey, known as "Sabbatai Zvi"[4] proclaimed he was the Messiah and convinced thousands of Jews to sell their belongings and go with him to the promised land.[5]

Jewish mysticism would seem far away from the Albanian scene, but there was a connection when the Turkish Sultan had to contend with Sabbatai Zvi. In Turkey, Zvi boasted that his army of followers would conquer Istanbul.

The Ottoman Empire was at its peak when the Sultan first had Zvi arrested for creating unrest in the Empire. The Sultan offered Zvi a choice between death or conversion to Islam, Zvi elected conversion.

When he converted, Nathan of Gaza, a famous Jewish traveler of that period, rationalized, "it was to penetrate into the depth of realm of evil in order to free the sparks imprisoned there." Several thousand of Zvi's followers also converted to Islam and two decades later other Jews converted to a Jewish-Moslem sect called "Donmeh." However, the majority of his followers remained Jews.

The Grand Vizir, in the year 1647, banished Zvi to Ulqin, a city on the Dalmatian coast. This was in spite of the fact Zvi had converted to Islam and had taken the name Aziz Mehmed Effendi.

At some point Zvi must have left Ulqin because in 1673 the Sultan exiled him to Albania a second time. This time he stayed in Albania and lived out his last days in Berat, dying in 1676. All that is known for sure about his tomb is that it was buried on the side of the river Osum, in central Albania.

His assumed burial place, near Berat, is treated as a holy place for all religions, and an annual fair is held on the site. The Universal Jewish Encyclopedia says Zvi's followers established themselves in Berat, and stayed for 30 years with a Salonika rabbi as the head of the community.

Zvi's assumed tomb became a shrine for an Islamic sect known as "Bektashi." Until 1965 it was common for Bektashi Moslems to make pilgrimages to this tomb.

In a remote village, in southern Albania, there is evidence of Jewish life dating from 500 years ago. It's possible Sabbatai Zvi spent his exile there, and it's possible that the people of the village of Ftera are descendants of his followers.

In 1956 an Israeli researcher found a letter written by Zvi, about six weeks before his death, asking the Jews of Berat to send him a prayer book for the high Jewish holidays. The letter is on exhibit at the Museum of Jerusalem. This is the only letter of Zvi ever found and it may be the only letter he ever wrote. According to an Israeli historian, the letter was found among pages of a book which belonged to a sect of his disciples living in Salonika, who publicly practiced the Islamic religion but actually practiced an illegal heretic form of Judaism.

Sabbatai Zvi had the distinction of being the most famous non-Albanian Jew to live in Albania, but he was not the only one. 250 years later, hundreds, if not thousands, of non-Albanian Jews would seek sanctuary in Albania.[6]

Footnotes:

1. In a travel book, published in 1934 (Albanian Journey, Bernard Newman, Pitman & Sons, London,) the writer refers to Spanish speaking Jewish merchants in Tirana. They probably were speaking Ladino. This has to be the exception that proves the rule. Few Albanian Jews know Ladino, a language spoken mostly in Turkey and Greece. The vast majority of Albanian Jews were living in Vlora and not Tirana at this time.

2. According to Edward Mantus, Bernstein had made arrangements with King Zog to have Jews from Austria and Germany settle in Albania. Letter to Editor, Jewish Chronicle, June 8, 1973.

3. See, Bernstein, Herman "Jews in Albania," Jewish Daily Bulletin, April 17 and 18, 1934.

4. There is no fixed way to spell his name.

5. Albanian Catholic Bulletin 1994, vol. XV, p.154.

6. Jacob Frank, a Sabbatai follower, claimed to be the reincarnation of Zvi. His followers were the Frankists. He was outcast from Judaism and responded by converting into the Roman Catholic church. This was the only time in history that a Jewish group claimed the blood libel was true.

Note: The Encyclopedia Judaica devotes 14 pages to Sabbatai and Sabbataism.

Chapter Four

In Moslem Albania During the Ottoman Period

Albania was a part of the Ottoman Empire for more than 400 years ending with Albanian Independence in 1912. From before the Second Wave and before the expulsion from Spain the Jews were under Moslem rule. The result is not what might have been expected.

Anyone who professed a belief in one God and was willing to accept the political supremacy of the Moslems was known as a "Dhimmi" and was afforded the protection of the Ottoman Empire and was not subject to persecution. This didn't mean, however, that the Christian, Armenian or Jew was equal to the Moslem under the law, far from it.

The Moslem had a higher status, paid lower taxes, and had greater opportunities than the non-Moslem. The Dhimmi, be he Jew or Christian, was subject to minor humiliations, but he did not have to fear pogroms or forced conversions.

The status of the Jew was on a par with the Christian and it doesn't appear that there was a distinction made between the various Dhimmi. In Christian Spain, Jews had been categorized with the Moslem minority. Now in Moslem Albania, and in the great Ottoman Empire the Jew was categorized with the Christian minority. A Jew was in a safer position as a Dhimmi under the Moslem Empire than he was under Christian rule during most of the four hundred years of the Ottoman Empire.

There is little mention of Jews in Albanian Government, military, or politics, although there is a record of a Jewish judge in 1903. During the Ottoman period this was

consistent with the Jew's status as a Dhimmi which didn't change after the Ottoman period. Whether this was intentional or whether it was just the fact they were so few, the Jews of Albania maintained a very low profile. There is very little mention of Jews in the usual histories of the country.

That there were poor Jews and rich Jews, educated Jews and uneducated Jews, may have contributed to the low profile. The only clustering related to housing, and even there the numbers weren't large enough to cause envy or resentment.

Independence Movements
The Greek aspirations for independence from Ottoman rule was a noble objective, but as in many other independence movements, the Jews got caught in the middle. The Greeks, in their anti-Turk, anti-Moslem movements, often equated Jews with Moslems with the Jews experiencing murder and mayhem. We can speculate on the reasons.

This could be attributed to the Jews' close association with the Moslems, a negative feeling towards all non-Greeks, traditional anti-Semitism, or all of the above. In Moslem-Christian confrontations in this part of the world Jews fared better under Moslem than under Christian rule. The best example is that during the two centuries of crusades Jews were murdered by the crusaders without reason.

Except for one or two bad periods, and during rebellions that were movements for independence from the Turks, Jews were safe from pogroms. It is paradoxical that it was the periods during which the Albanians were attempting to attain their political freedom from the Ottoman that we find massacre of Jews. Whether or not Jews merely wanted the preservation of the status quo or were loyal to the Ottoman, they were perceived as being pro-Ottoman and therefore was considered the enemy of the national independence movements.

For example, when the Albanians (Greeks) revolted against the Turks in 1911 there were accusations that the Jews sided with the Turks, resulting in the murder of Jews by "Patriots."

Historically it has been the Jewish practice to accept the political force in power. Jews weren't revolutionaries by nature, at least not until the end of the 19th and beginning of the 20th centuries. This could be attributed to an attitude of "the devil you know is better than the devil you don't know" or to Jewish experience that the Jew remains a persecuted minority regardless of the political administration, so why get involved in something that doesn't directly concern him? This may have been an attitude of "let the gentiles fight among themselves, the Jew is a Jew regardless of who wins the political fight." Years of revolutions and changes of government and extreme nationalism have not been good years for Jews.

Jews had been loyal to the Ottoman and appreciated that their status and freedom from fear was greater under the Turk than under most other European governments. The Jews suffered for their support of Ottoman rule. In their unsuccessful rebellions against the Turks the Greeks would often take their frustrations out against the Jews.

The Millet System
Albania was a part of the Ottoman Empire for four hundred years. The full occupation was complete by 1501 and lasted until 1912. The Ottoman used what they called the "Millet System" to administer its far reaching territorial empire.

The Millet was a self governing organization based on religion with the religious leaders having both secular and religious authority. Everything was controlled by the rabbis in Jewish Millet except economics, which was controlled by the merchant and craft guilds.

Within the Millet, Jews could worship in their own way and speak their own language and pretty much control their own lives as long as they kept the peace and paid their taxes. There is the argument that the Millet system fostered hostility among the ethnic groups isolating them to keep them from joining together against the ruling Turks. That's probably true, which made Millits even more desirable from the Ottoman point of view.

The Millet system was used throughout the Ottoman Empire for non-Moslems. The most important minorities under this system were Greek Orthodox, Armenians, and Jews (Palestine). The Millet was an expression of Turk tolerance, but it was also an expedient way to administer a large empire. The system didn't break up until the end of the Second World War, although it ended in Albania in 1912

Jews in the Ottoman Army
In the period from 1855 onward Jews paid a "Military Substitution Tax" instead of serving in the Ottoman army. The tax was abolished in 1910 and Jews became subject to the draft. Most Jews served willingly in the Albanian army although some fled to Greece to avoid military service. The army provided kosher food and permitted the Jewish soldiers to observe their holidays.

We know of at least one Albanian Jewish doctor who served in the Ottoman army. Dr. Solomon Efendi was a military doctor who began his career in 1896-97.

Corfu
Iberian and Italian Jews have lived on the island of Corfu since the 12th century, under the Venetians and Ottoman. Jewish life had evolved into separate Italian and Greek Jewish communities. Jews lived in peace and prosperity on Corfu in these two rival communities until the Greek revolutions.

It was only when the Greeks, during their anti-Turk revolutions, threatened the entire Jewish population that the two groups of Jews banded together out of absolute necessity.

Large numbers of Jews on Corfu and elsewhere were massacred by the Greeks in their revolution of 1821, even though Jews had no significant part in Turkish rule and were bystanders in Moslem-Christian confrontations. The records of the massacres read like the 20th century Holocaust: 5,000 Jews were murdered in Morea, hundreds were killed in Wallachia, 1200 Jews were murdered in Tripoliza. The Jews living on the Islands of Sparta, Patras, Corinthos, Mistra, and Argos were wiped out. The same was true of the Jews of Thebes, Vrachori, Attica, and Epirus.

At first Corfu was the objective for Jews fleeing from the bands of Greek rebels, but this island proved to be anything except a safe haven. Gangs of Greeks massacred large numbers of Jews on Corfu. The sanctuary for the Jews was Izmir in Turkey where a new Jewish community was formed.

Only in northern Greece, in the areas of Janina and Salonika, were Jews and Turks able to resist the Greeks and avoid the massacres. At this time (1820) Janina was the capitol of the Vilayet of Janina, one of the four provinces created by the Turks that constituted Greater Albania.

In 1891 the "Blood Libel" raised its ugly head in Corfu and there were anti-Jewish riots, so many Jews moved to Janina.[1]

During the Greek-Turkish war of 1897 the Jews of Corfu and the Greek mainland were subject to persecutions and murder, causing additional migrations to Ottoman controlled Salonika and Izmir. It didn't help the Jews in

their relation with the Greeks that in the prior year there was a newspaper report that the Sultan honored the chief rabbi of Janina.

In 1909, a band of Greek-Albanians killed four Jews and wounded several others. They cut off the ears of their victims and sent them to the synagogue.[2] This was said to be revenge for Jews carrying out espionage against the Greek revolutionaries.

In the 1911 Albanian revolt, the Jews were accused of collaborating with the Turks to suppress the revolution which ultimately brought independence to Albania.

In 1912 the Ottoman Empire was falling apart. The Balkans were a series of small nations, each suspicious of the others. The Serbs wanted access to the sea, something which Austria opposed. The Austrians felt that an independent Albania was preferable as it would block Serbia from the sea. From this was born a liberated Albania. Independence served the Albanians well, as they were able to remain neutral during the First World War, even though a portion of the country was occupied by Italian, Austro-Hungarian, and French troops.

Footnotes:
1. Jewish Chronicle, May 29, 1891, p.7. The "Blood Libel" is an ancient fiction that the Jews killed gentile children to get their blood for some religious purposes.
2. Jewish Chronicle, January 29, 1909, p.8.

Chapter Five

The Inter War Period

Albania was proclaimed an independent state in 1912 and was able to remain neutral during the First World War, but it was a battlefield for the warring nations.(1) By secret agreement in 1915 the Allies carved up the territory of Albania putting some areas occupied almost totally by Albanians outside the country's borders. It wasn't until 1920 that the Albanians were able to force the Italians from their land.

In 1923, the great powers drew new boundaries and separated half the country and half its people from Albania.

In June, 1924, the Government was run by the first democratic statesman of Albania, Bishop Fan S. Noli, and Albania was admitted to the League of Nations the same year. Noli's government lasted only six months. In December, 1924, the country was taken over by a dictator, A. B. Zogolli, who was known as Zog. He proclaimed himself President in 1924, and in 1928, named himself King.

The period between the World Wars was one of great prosperity for Albanian Jews, but it was also a period of weakening of Jewish traditions. The only synagogue was destroyed and was never rebuilt. The matriarch of the Levi family was going to pay for the rebuilding of the synagogue but died before it could be built. The last Jewish school closed during this period.

Jakoel called the period from 1925 until 1939, the period of rule by King Zog, "A golden age for Jews in Albania," even though the Jewish community wasn't officially recognized by the Albanian Government until April 2, 1937.

In the 1930s the municipality of Vlora adopted an ordinance requiring that Jewish owned stores be open on Saturday and closed on Sunday.[2] Heavy fines were imposed for violation of this law. The first Saturday after the law was enacted the Jewish shops stayed closed and the fines were imposed. The fine was increased the second week. The decision among those store owners who had limited resources was to remain open on Saturdays but not to sell anything. The more prosperous merchants kept their stores closed and paid the fines.

The Jewish store keepers sued the municipality of Vlora and the Albanian courts agreed with the Jews that they could close on Saturdays, and the courts made the municipality return the collected fines.

In 1927 the "small number" of Albanian Jews lived primarily in Korça, according to the Encyclopedia Judaica. There is a difference of opinion as to the location of the main portion of the Jewish community during the interwar period. Jakoel challenged this and said the majority of the Jews were living in Vlora. In the 1930 census there were 204 Jews living in Albania. According to official records the Jewish population of Albania in 1937 was 120, residing mostly in Vlora and Delvina.

In 1928, the Albanian constitution was amended to include a statement of religious freedom. It stated: "All religions and faiths are honored and their liberty of practice assured. Religion can in no way form judicial barriers. Religion cannot be used for political purposes."

The Albanian state has no official religion. All religions and faiths were honored, and their liberty of practice was assured. Religion was not permitted to form jurisdictional barriers and religious proselytizing was forbidden. The 1939 Revised Constitution stated that all religions are to be respected and their external practices guaranteed by law.

Janina (Ioanina)

Although Janina and nearby Preveza [3] are currently within Greece, their place in Albanian-Jewish history is assured. Janina remained under Ottoman rule from October 9, 1430, until 1913, when the Janina District, which had been a part of Albania, became a part of Greece.

Most Romaniot Jews can trace their family history to Janina. The Greek spoken by the Jews in this area was so archaic that it suggests there is truth to the claim that there was a Jewish community in Janina as far back as the 9th century. Janina was capital of its region and a wealthy town in which Jews and others prospered.

There were golden days in Janina but there were also pogroms. For example, there is a newspaper account of large numbers of Jews murdered in Janina on January 29, 1909.

Calculating the size of the Jewish population of Janina is difficult because it varied in size during various periods. The calculation is further complicated by the fact that sometimes the census is reported in terms of families, and other times in terms of individuals. The years of the biggest growth were the years when the Ottoman welcomed the refugees from the Spanish Inquisition, who were assimilated into the Romaniot population. The years of the greatest shrinkage of population were during the period between 1912 and 1920, when many Albanians emigrated to the United States, and of course the black day in March, 1944, when the Holocaust arrived in Janina.

In 1831, there was a community of 212 families which increased to 343 families by 1856. With an average of six per family this amounted to 1200 and 2056 respectively. In 1870, there was a shrinkage to 250 families (1500 people) which may be explained by the large number who migrated to Vlora. In the next six years (1876) there was a doubling of population to 3,000. The Jewish population remained at the 3,000 level until the years of great migration to the United States mentioned earlier.

On the eve of the Holocaust there were 1950 Jews living in Janina. In one day, in 1944 (March 24), 1860 Jews were sent to Auschwitz. In 1948, their number was 170. There are less than 100 Jews in Janina today.

The Jews of Janina possessed an old torah claimed to be at least 1500 years old known as the "Safer (book) of Vlora" formerly belonging to the Jews of Vlora. Inscriptions on the torah would indicate there were Jews in that area more than 1500 years earlier. In 1936, the Albanians requested the return of the torah, but the Jews of Janina kept postponing the return. The old torah was burned by the Nazis with the other torahs found in Janina.

The Four Vilayets
To understand the relation of Janina to Albania in general, and to Vlora in particular, it's necessary to understand the four Vilayets during the period of the Ottoman Empire.

Until 1878 Greater Albania was divided into four "Vilayets" or provinces or districts: Janina, Shkodra, Kosova and Manastir. Janina was the capital of the Vilayet of Janina.(4) Not only was Janina in Albania, but it was in the same district as Berat and Vlora. This facilitated movement between Janina and Vlora and ultimately to the emigration which constituted the Third Wave.

By the end of the 19th century the ties between Vlora and Janina were still strong but were weakened from what they had been. The Vilayets had been abolished and Janina was now Greek, even though it was still not completely free of the Ottoman Empire.

At the same time there was a strengthening of the ties between the Jews of Corfu and Vlora. Corfu is very close to Vlora and the ties would have been stronger except for the language difficulty. The Jews of Corfu tended to speak an Italianized version of Greek. Hebrew wasn't a common language during this period, as the great revival of Hebrew as a spoken language hadn't yet occurred.

FOUR ALBANIAN VILAYETS DURING THE OTTOMAN EMPIRE (until 1878)

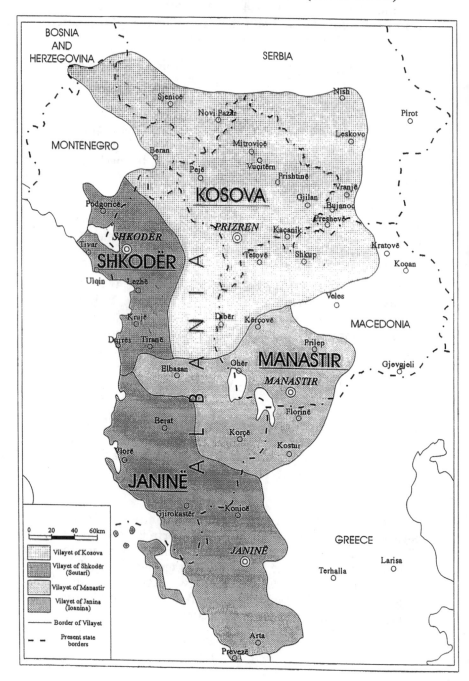

There was a post World War II link between the Jews of Albania and Janina but it was a weak one. Only 10% of the Jews of Janina survived and Hoxha's isolationist policies contributed, but the final break in the link was when the Jews of Albania emigrated to Israel.

As devastated as they were in Janina, the Janina Relief Fund sent 1,500 pounds of Matzo flour to the Albanians, in 1945. In March, 1953, the Janina Relief Fund provided aid to what they call the "Janina Jews living in Albania."

After the First World War there was a war between Greece and Turkey. Many Jews from Janina went to Albania to avoid being drafted into the Greek army.

Footnotes:
1. Albania was the last Balkan state to become independent of Turkey.
2. At the same time there were similar court cases in Poland and New York. Those cases went one step further and involved Jewish owned stores opening on Sunday. The Albanian court held that all stores must be closed on Sunday, even though the sabbath for the majority of the population was Friday, the Moslem sabbath.
3. Much of what is written about Janina has application to Preveza, but to a lesser extent.
4. After the defeat of Turkey by Russia in 1878, Albania, still a part of the Ottoman Empire, was fragmented and substantially reduced in size. Part of each Vilayet was ceded to a neighboring country. For our interests the most important change is that Janina was no longer in Albania, and Vlora remained the center of Jewish life in Albania.

Chapter Six

Jewish Refugees

The first Jewish refugees in modern times came to Albania in 1933, mostly from Germany and Austria en-route to the United States, South America, Turkey and elsewhere. Few, if any, planned to stay. Albania was a convenient way station on the road to someplace else.

As more and more German and Austrian Jews became apprehensive of their future under the Nazis regime the numbers attempting to escape from Europe steadily increased. During the first months of 1939 the Albanian consulates were flooded with Jews seeking visas. At first the applicants for visas were mainly from German and Austrian Jews but by the end of 1938, and the start of 1939, they were joined by others from Central Europe.

Getting a visa to enter Albania as a transit point out of Europe wasn't difficult as the Albanian Government was very liberal in granting and extending transit visas. The problem wasn't in getting into Albania, it was finding a place beyond.

As the numbers of Jews entering Albania increased the available destinations decreased. There were international conferences attended by representatives of the United States, Italy and Albania, looking for places for the Jewish refugees. Even Italy offered to take 5,000 Jewish refugees in their African colonies. In the winter of 1938-39 the United State quota system made it impossible for more Jews to gain entry. The conferences ended after achieving very little.

At the start of 1938 there were 300 Albanian Jews living in the country.[1] During 1938 and 1939 the Jewish

population increased substantially. There was an increase in the numbers entering Albania at a time when there was a decrease in the numbers leaving. By the end of 1938 the number of Jews had officially increased to 350, but there were many more Jews in the country, mostly with expired "tourist" or "transit" visas.

Ambassador Bernstein arranged for Austrian and German Jews to settle in Albania. For example, in February, 1939, 100 Jews who came from Vienna were allowed to legally settle in Albania, 60 in Tirana and 40 in Durrës.

An additional 95 Jewish families arrived in March, 1939. King Zog allowed the Jews to settle in his country, but he fled for his own life to Greece less than a month later, after the Italians invaded Albania on April 7th, Good Friday.

With the Italian invasion of Albania, in April, and the start of the global war in September, 1939, the refugees had to accept the fact they were in Albania for the duration of the War. Things were so good for the Albanian Jews and they felt so secure, that little attention was paid to the admonitions of the emigrants about the growing horrors in Central Europe.

Things became very confused about where Jews were safe. At one time the escape route was from Albania to Italy and beyond. After the war started there were German Jews who were able to get to Italy, and from there illegally to Albania.

The number of Jewish refugees stranded in Albania was measured in the hundreds, if not thousands. But they were stranded in a country of which Ambassador Bernstein had written, "There is no trace of any discrimination against them (Jews) in Albania because Albania happens to be one of the rare lands in Europe today where religious prejudice and hate do not exist."

Albanian Government

The Albanian Government adopted various anti-Jewish regulations in the 1938-39 period, even before the Italian invasion. But the Albanian Government had neither the will nor the time to enforce these regulations. The ostensible reason for the regulations was to appease the Italians, who were aware of the Jews in Albania and the fact that they were virtually unrestricted.

The restrictions imposed on Jews included a limitation of tourist visas to 30 days. The tourist visas were "tourist" in name only. That was the way the Jews entered Albania, and once they entered, they sought a way to leave. When it became impossible to leave, the "tourist" became an illegal resident of Albania.

The Albanian counsels abroad were instructed to refrain from issuing tourist visas to Jews but they continued to do so until the start of the World War. Many counsels simply ignored the restrictions. After the World War started some Jews were still able to get visas too enter Albania, although bribes were necessary in some cases.

Financial and Other Support

Although they were stranded in Albania, the Jewish refugees were relatively safe. But most soon saw their available funds dissipated. The local Jewish communities came to their aide through the good efforts of some wealthy Jewish merchants, Isaac Kohan, in Durrës, and Rafael Levi, and Rafael Jakoel, in Vlora. The majority of the funds were provided by Jewish welfare organizations including the American Joint Distribution Committee. There was even a small amount of aid to the needy refugees from the Albanian Government.

Jews who had been in Albania for several months were permitted to work at their trades and professions and were given residency permits. The official policy was that the refugees must leave Albania when their visas expired, but this rule was honored by its breach. Meanwhile the

34

Albanian counsels were facilitating the movement of Jews into Albania. In spite of official policy the counsels continued to issue visas.

After the invasion the Italians put pressure on the Albanian Government to expel the foreign Jews and to initiate additional restrictions on Jews. The Albanians resisted this pressure and not a single Jew was expelled.

Italy and the Italian Occupation
Italy was the only country with which Albania had a treaty and it was Italy that invaded Albania in April, 1939. This may explain Albania's reluctance to enter into a treaty since the World War.

The Italians sometimes referred to anti-Semitism as the "German disease" and even when they did the Germans bidding, they did it halfheartedly. In Italy, the Jews were relatively secure until Italy capitulated in November, 1943, and the central and northern parts of the country (including Rome) came under German occupation. Tragically, these were the areas of the greatest concentration of Italian Jews.

The Italians were rarely willing tools of the Germans with respect to the Jewish question. We know from the testimony of people who were there that life in the Italian administered camps in Yugoslavia was bearable and that Italian soldiers assisted Yugoslavian Jews in escaping to Albania. This was at a time when large numbers of Jews from all over Europe were being transported to Poland to the German death camps.

When the Italians arrived in Albania they announced some anti-Jewish rules. Jews were cut off from cultural, social and political activities. In comparison to other occupied countries the restrictions were rather insignificant.

During the period of the Italian occupation of Albania many Jewish refugees led ordinary lives without hiding

their identity. They celebrated the Jewish Holy Days and worked for their living at what they could, but things changed rapidly when Italy surrendered and joined the Allies in the autumn of 1943. The Germans came to Albania. Some 800 Jewish refugees from Yugoslavia, Bulgaria, Germany, Poland and Austria living in Albania once again faced fear and the need to find a hiding place.

In the last days of the Italian occupation the Italians were ordered to round up the Jews in Albania to concentrate them all in one place, an American agricultural school in Kavaja. We know what usually followed.

The Italian soldiers guarding the Jews were to be replaced by German soldiers. The Italian Commandant, ostensibly, opened the gates of the school and told the Jews to scatter. What makes this story plausible, is the fact that nothing has been found which would indicate there was anything approaching a concentration camp in Albania and we know there was no "transportation" of Jews from Albania to the death camps.

Jakoel said that sometimes he finds it difficult to know how to judge the Italians. When they came they instituted restrictions on the Jews and seemed to want to humiliate them, but they didn't stop Jews from having gainful employment. The Italians who came in contact with Jews generally treated them without discrimination.

When Rafael Jakoel was arrested for helping guerrillas, local Italians testified on his behalf even though they knew the charges were true.

When Italy surrendered the Albanian partisans had a windfall, as several hundred Italian soldiers joined them, bringing a large amount of arms and military equipment. An unknown, but smaller number of Italian soldiers joined the German forces.

The Annexed Territories

In April, 1941, the territory of Kosova,[2] then a part of Yugoslavia and inhabited mostly by ethnic Albanians, was annexed to Albania and put under "Albanian control," which was really Italian control.

First the Germans imposed laws for persecuting Jews, the same laws they had instituted in the other occupied countries. These were not applicable to Albania proper. For example, Jews in the annexed territories were required to wear a "J" or "Jew"on their clothes. These laws were unknown in Albania proper.

The Jews in the "annexed area" were not as fortunate as the Jews in Albania proper. Life in the annexed territories was not as secure and there were unfortunate incidents of Jews being abused by the local people.

Jews from Serbia and Croatia had fled to this area and these refugees were relatively well treated by the Albanians and Italians, until the Italians began to comply with German demands regarding the Jews. This compares unfavorably with the experience in Albania proper where the Albanians refused to provide lists of Jews and didn't cooperate in arresting Jews.

In Prishtina, capital city of the annexed territories, the local authorities complied with German demands and jailed 60 Jewish men. A sympathetic doctor, Spiro Lit, convinced the mayor that they must not let the Germans take the 60 Jews to Poland for extermination. He also convinced the German authorities that the Jewish prisoners had typhus and it was necessary to send the Jews to hospitals in Albania to avoid an epidemic. The Jews were taken to Berat, given false documents and spread around Albania, mostly to the friends of Dr. Lito in the cities of Lushnja, Shijak, Kavaja, and Kruja.

The Albanian Minister of Interior gave some instructions to the Prefect of Police of the annexed territories that tells a

story with a partial happy ending. The motivation isn't clear, but some lives were saved.

An order from the Minister dated March 20, 1942, directed: "All the Jews that have been in your region before the separation of Yugoslavia should be transferred within 3 days to Berat. They should not be stopped on their way. If they do not firmly follow the instructions, they should be told they will be deported. The Jews who came after the war started should be kept in prison and you should make a list of their names."

The Minister apparently changed his mind because 10 days later (April 1, 1942) he revised his instructions: "The Jews who came after the war started should not be imprisoned but should be gathered on a *field of concentration*, because there may be women and children among them. You should coordinate with the military authorities to find a common plan for the whole of Kosova. For those who have been here before the war, you should stop deporting to Berat until further orders."

The Prefect of Police didn't work very fast and on May 20, he notified the Minister: "The Jews are gathered in a *field of concentration* in the central part of our prefecture being always under observation."

Two days later the Minister again revised his instructions: "About the Jews who were in that region before the war, the men should be sent to Berat. Women and children should be free to stay where they are or go to Berat. If anyone who is supposed to be sent to Berat is ill, wait until his recovery."

On July 5, some Jews must still have been in prison because the Minister directed: "The Jews who are in your prison should be separated into four groups and sent to Kavaja, Kruja, Burrel and Shijak, where they will live under close observation by the police. Every person or family is free to chose who he wants in his group, except that each group should have about the same number of people."

The order doesn't say "Jews who came after the war started" it just says "Jews who are in prisons." But in 1942, it was probable that the Jews in prison were those who arrived after the war started and were in the country illegally.

It's paradoxical that there was concern for the sick, an appreciation of the need to keep families together, and a concern for women and children at the same time they are talking about the *field of concentration*, and eventually complied with German demands for Jewish prisoners. The good result was that those who went to Berat and the four towns mentioned (Kavaja, Kruja, Burrel, and Shijak) were in Albania and Albania meant life but not everyone was so fortunate.

There was inconsistencies and a lack of formality that was confusing to the "inmates" of these *fields of concentration* and to those trying to understand the situation half a century later.

There were barbed wire fences surrounding these *fields of concentration* and there were Italian guards, yet there was testimony of Jews going to Kavaja to a cinema or a football match or to celebrate Jewish holidays. This inconsistent pattern suggests two things. First, the guards and camp officials either didn't have firm instructions or were unwilling to carry them out. Second, we can't generalize from the few reports of experience in these camps as the conditions varied substantially from place to place and from time to time.

In June, 1943, while still under Italian control, the Albanian police chief suggested the jailing of certain Jews: "According to our investigation the Jews listed below are dangerous because they are propaganderizing against the Axis (Rome-Berlin) and they want to organize actions and hold meetings. We think these people should be taken away from here as soon as possible to one of the concentration fields, because their staying here could be dangerous to the regime."

Not every Jew in the annexed territories was lucky enough to be relocated to Albania proper. There was an unknown number of Jewish refugees held in the prison in Prishtina. The Italians turned them over to the Germans who took them to Belgrade where they were killed. It's very likely that these were the Jews that the police chief described as dangerous. In April, 1944, the Germans shipped 400 Jews from the annexed territories to Bergen-Belsen; 100 survived the war.

According to one report the survival rate in Kosove was sixty percent, which made it, relatively, one of the areas with the highest percentage of survival in occupied Europe.

Footnotes:
1. Ambassador Bernstein habitually understated the numbers of Jews in Albania. For example, he wrote, "There are only one hundred Jews in the entire country." We can assume he did this purposefully.
2. The status of Kosova, currently a part of Yugoslavia, is in contention today. Albanians favor either Independence for Kosova or its being a part of Albania. The people of the area are ethnic Albanians.

* * * *

Some Case Notes

Note A
Report June 30, 1943 of the Police Office of Prishtina
Solomon Hazmonay
Father's name Haim, mother's name Sara, born in Bulgaria in 1913, citizen of Sofia. Asked why he entered Albania illegally: "On June 6 we left Skopje on a wagon (railroad car) used to carry animals and we came to Fenicaj on June 7. When we got off the train we were caught by the police and sent to jail. The reason we came here is that the Bulgarian authorities wanted to confiscate our wealth and deport us. We came to Albania to escape from danger. We have only a few dollars." We don't know what happened to this family, but we do know that the Albanian Government did provide a small stipend for needy refugee families.

Note B
Report of an unnamed women living in the territories. She was complaining that she was arrested by mistake. Although she was born a Jew she had converted early in life and had married a Christian and felt that she wasn't a Jew. No record was found of the disposition of her plea, but if it was handled in the usual manner her plea was to no avail.

Note C
The Fields of Concentration
This was the name given to what were otherwise known as concentration camps. These were camps for civilians and although their populations were mainly Jews there were other "trouble makers" put in the camps. The camps were surrounded by barbed wire and Italian soldiers. Disease in the camps was rampant and uncontrollable. The Barracks were wooden and without windows. The beds were also wooden and three tiered. It was an ugly place.

Chapter Seven

The Germans

Request for list of Jews
In late 1943, the Germans requested that the Jewish leaders provide a list of Jews living in Albania. This seemingly innocent request was later known to be the first step in transporting Jews to the concentration camps. The Jews did not supply the list in 1943 but there was fear, in 1944, that the Regency would comply with the German request.

In the spring of 1944 the Nazis officially asked the Regency for a list of all Jews, and that they be gathered in one place.

Josef Jakoel's father, Rafael Jakoel, and his uncle Mateo Matalia became aware of the German intention to arrest all Jews in Albania. As leaders of the Jewish community they appealed to one of the Regents, Mehdi Frashëri. He recommended they contact the Minister of the Interior, Xhafer Deva, who was reputed to be anti-Semitic.

The Jewish delegation knew they were risking their lives in going to see Minister Deva, and told their families of the possibility they would not be returning. To their joy, the Minister's nationalism exceeded his anti-Semitism and he agreed with the Jews and protested to the Germans. Deva was able to get the Germans to accept his rejection of their request for the lists.

Memories fade and time takes its toll. There is another version of this story, with Deva denying the German request, and then informing the Jewish leadership that the Germans accepted his decision and it wasn't necessary to supply the list. It matters little which version is accepted as the result was the same, i.e. the Albanians stood up to the Nazis and denied them the list.

When Minister Deva refused the request he reportedly told the Germans that he considered the request a flagrant violation of their agreement and an interference with the internal affairs of Albania. He told the representatives of the Jewish community about his response to the request of the Nazis, and he assured them that as long as the Albanian Government had any power they had nothing to be afraid of. The subsequent events showed the veracity of this statement.

The fact that the Albanian Government and people did not cooperate with the Germans did not mean there was no danger to the Jews, or to the Moslems and Christians who protected them. All around them, in Corfu, Janina and in the annexed territories, Jews were being transported to the death camps. The importance of denying the request for the list of the Jews cannot be overstated. There definitely was a correlation between the denial of a list and the rate of survival. A good example was in nearby Greece. A list was provided in Solonika and there was a survival rate of 10%. In Athens the Jews refused to supply a list and there was a 50% survival rate.

Negotiations
Jakoel tells of the experience when he and three other young Jewish men were being sought by the Gestapo. The other three were captured by the Nazis, and the "elders" of the Vlora Jewish community tried to negotiate their release. They approached the Gestapo chief through an intermediary. In the meantime, one of the three got a message out to his brother saying his destiny was sealed but to be careful for the rest of the family. The representative of General Futzstun, the Gestapo chief, made an offer to release the four Jews upon payment of a considerable amount of money. The only guarantee that the German would keep the bargain was the "word of honor" of the Gestapo chief. When the bribe was paid the four Jews were released.

There was a similar incident involving a Jew, Pepe Levi, who refused to work as an informant for the Germans. He felt doomed and said goodbye to his family when he went to tell the Germans his decision. For whatever reason, after hearing his rejection of the demand that he be an informant, the Germans let him go. The only explanation is that the end was near for the Third Reich and although the Germans were speeding up their killing machines, individual German officers didn't want their name linked with killing a specific named Jew.

There was one final incident that could have meant the end of the Jews of Vlora. The Nazis had prepared a list, including addresses, and planned to arrest all the Jews in the morning of the day they would leave Vlora. They knew the end was near. On the day before the Germans planned departure, the partisans came down from the hills and surrounded the city. The partisans began to sing and dance as was their custom before they would begin an attack, as a form of psychological warfare. The Germans decided to depart that night instead of the following morning. This saved the lives of the Jews of Vlora.

Chapter Eight

The Righteous and the Holocaust

Now that Albania is "open" we learn for the first time the remarkable story of Albanians protecting Jews during the Italian and German occupations. The thrilling story of the rescue of the Jews of Denmark is well known, acknowledged, and appreciated. The story of the rescue of Jews in Albania was buried for four decades due to the isolationist and anti-Israel policies of a Communist dictator.

Every Albanian Jew survived the Holocaust. Every Greek, Yugoslav, Austrian and German Jew who was lucky enough to get into Albania proper also survived. The Albanian story is all the more remarkable for the fact that the majority of the Righteous rescuers were Moslems, although there were Eastern Orthodox and Roman Catholic rescuers as well.

Another remarkable fact is that no instance was found where an Albanian accepted compensation for hiding Jews.

Although there hasn't yet been a statistical study of the country of origin, the majority of the hidden foreign Jews were from the bordering country of Yugoslavia. The importance of Albania as a sanctuary is demonstrated by the fact that less than 10% of Yugoslavia's 70,000 Jews survived the Holocaust.[1]

There were additional ways in which the situation in Albania was different from other occupied countries. The time period during which the Jews were in serious jeopardy was relatively short, from autumn, 1943, to October, 1944. Like no other occupied country, Albania had more Jews within its borders at the end of the war than at the beginning.

45

While the devil ran amok in the surrounding countries of Europe, Albania was like what one survivor called the "Garden of Eden" for Jewish refugees. The following is an example of the experiences of a refugee family from Yugoslavia.

When the Germans put their race laws into practice, this family with false identities, escaped to Southern Yugoslavia, at that time under Italian control. The Italians arrested them for illegal entry, and put them in a prison camp with other Jewish families. The Italians were humane in their treatment of the Jews in these family camps, and sometimes it was possible for the men to work in their trades or professions. Sometimes the Jewish children within these camps played games with the children of the guards.

The big problems started when there were complaints about over crowding in the camp. When the Jews complained the Italians relayed the message to the Germans who seemed willing to cooperate. The next day the Germans came and took half of the population of the camp to a forest near Prishtina and killed them. This was in a part of Yugoslavia which the Germans had annexed to Albania, the so-called Annexed Territories.

The Italians apparently felt guilty about this and smuggled the remaining Jews to Albania, which, at the time, was occupied solely by Italians. The Jews were smuggled across the border in food transport trucks, hiding them between sacks of food.

With hell breaking loose in Europe, they were going to another world - a mythical island, that was Albania! When the people of Albania extended their traditional hospitality the Jews saw the contrast between Hell and Heaven.

Naftali told his story: "I was then a boy of 14. We escaped from occupied Serbia through Bulgaria to the province of

Kosobo, (in the annexed territories) where we met a horrible reception. The Germans put pressure on the Italians to arrest Jews, and my family was arrested and put in prison. Then we saw Albanians at their best. A group of Albanian judges arrived and pretended to deport the refugees south into Albania. They did this to save our lives and transferred us to Kavaja, a small town in central Albania.

It was a market day when the three trucks full of Jews arrived in Kavaja. Mihal, who was 17 at the time, took my family to his family's small hotel and gave us food. They gave me a job washing dishes. Soon after we arrived the Germans came and it was necessary to transfer us to Tirana, but to do this required documents and traveling papers. You know the story of Mihal stealing the papers for us."

Mihal Lekatari's Story
In 1942 there were Jewish refugees freed from Italian jails who were moved to Kavaja. The Jewish families didn't have Albanian identification papers, which was a problem. Mihal Lekatari, an Orthodox Christian boy of 17, understood the danger facing the Jewish families.

Early one morning, Mihal armed himself and went to the police headquarters. He didn't expected any one would be there that early but found a secretary already at work. He took all the blank identity cards, about 50, and threatened the secretary with "death for you and your family if you report me."

Refik Veseli and others provided the necessary photos, but the identity cards weren't any good without the official embossing stamp. Mihal promptly returned to the police headquarters and stole the embossing stamp.

At the time this all occurred, Mihal was a student at the teachers college. Why did he do it? His answer almost half a century later is heartwarming: "There was no religious

reason for doing what I did. I tried to save Jews as they were human beings in terrible danger and I didn't care what their religion or nationality was. We loved them as human beings. Now I am very happy by the respect shown me by the Jewish people."

One of the users of these false papers still has the photo that had been attached to his "papers" and called it the nicest and most moving gift he ever received. He hugged Mihal and said "Gold, you and your family and the Albanian people are pure gold. It's not surprising Jews were saved from the train trip to death." Mihal has been honored as a Righteous Gentile.

The Veseli and Mandil Families
Moshe Mandil and his family fled from their native Belgrade and were relatively safe when interned in a southern Yugoslavia camp, which was under Italian control. After being interned by the Italians for more than a year, the Mandil family and 120 other Jews escaped to Albania.

The Jewish refugees lived in relative safety until the autumn of 1943 when the Germans replaced the Italians as occupiers of Albania. When the Germans took control, Refik Veseli decided that the 7 Jews he was hiding in Tirana would be safer at his parent's home in his native village. They were given forged documents, dressed in Albanian peasant cloth and were getting used to their new Moslem names. Refik decided it would be better to walk than to take a bus so the 7 Jews walked the 50 km to Kruja. Refik was afraid that if they were on the bus someone might identify them as Jews. At that time he wasn't sure how the Albanian people would have reacted. He didn't want to take unnecessary risks. In time he learned that there was little risk, if any, of the Albanian people reporting the presence of Jews.

The Mandil and the Ben-Yosef families, consisting of 5 adults and 2 children, were hidden in the house of Refik's

48

parents, in the mountain village of Kruja, until the war ended. Refik admits his parents had some initial hesitation about taking these strangers into their home, but in time they acknowledged that this was the proper thing to do.

In addition to the threat of being arrested by the Germans, there was the practical problem of having 7 strangers living in their home for a prolonged period. Refik's family gave the Jewish families shelter for an entire year. There was a cave about 50 meters from the Veseli house, and the Jewish adults retired to the cave when Germans came looking for Jews. Not once were they made to feel an unwelcome burden, and all financial compensation was refused.

After the war, Refik went to Belgrade to visit the Mandils, where he learned photography in Mandil's studio. Refik learned well and opened a photography studio of his own in Tirana.

Mandil started the letter writing campaign which resulted in Refik and his parents being honored by Yad Vashem as Righteous Among the Nations. They were the first Albanians, and among the first Moslems, honored by Yad Vashem. (See, Righteous Among the Nations)

Atif and Ganimet Toptani
Like many other Albanians the Toptani family was sympathetic to German culture and education, but not to the Nazis. Like many of the Righteous they were active in helping the Allied cause as well as protecting Jews.

During a German operation against partisan forces a British colonel, serving in the British Military Mission, was seriously wounded. He was taken to the village of Kamez, north of Tirana, to the house of the Toptani family who gave him shelter.

The Toptani family also sheltered the Levi and Altarac families in their home, even though they had never met the Jewish families before they opened their door to them. Edij

Toptani was 12 years old at the time and became a good friend of the Jewish children Jasha and Mica. Members of the Toptani family have been honored as Righteous Gentiles

Sulo Mecaj

Sulo Mecaj was a farmer in Kruja and lived with his wife and son in a small house he built with his father. In 1943 he opened his house to ten Jews, including the members of the Battino family. Sulo's son told what happened when the Germans came to Kruja. "My father received a message that the Germans were coming to our house looking for Jews. He told the Jews that when he gives a signal they should go to the crawl space that he had prepared for them in the attic. Panic surfaced and my father tried to reassure the Jews that it was unlikely they would be discovered. One Jew asked what would happen if the Germans set fire to the house. To reassure them, my father told me, his only son, to go into the attic with them and suffer their fate if the house is set on fire. My father had no choice. It was a matter of honor."

Sulo's son was asked how he felt about his father subjecting him to the risk of his life. The question bewildered and confused him. His reaction was that it was the proper thing to do so his father had no choice, it was a matter of honor. When asked whether he would have done as his father had done, his answer was "of course." Sulo's grandson, who was listening to the conversation, added his "of course." They both looked at me as if I had asked a foolish question, I had.

An event occurred in Kruja that threatened the Jews, and the Albanians that were protecting them. The village was liberated by the partisans and there was dancing in the streets, and the Jews came out of their hiding places. A few days later the Germans counterattacked and regained control of the village. All the villagers had seen the Jews come out of the Veseli, Mecaj, and other homes. It was a

worrisome time, but "Besa," the Albanian code of honor, controlled, and no one told the Germans about the Jews in the town.

If a villager had told the Germans about the Jews he would have been immediately executed, and his family would have been banished from the village, as this would have disgraced the family.

The Nosi Family (Vasil and his sister Adelina)
In March, 1943, the Macedonian Jews were taken to the Treblinka death camp. Marko Menahem, a Macedonian Jew, lost his entire family and escaped to Albania. He first went to Tirana, but when he was told the Germans were looking for him he fled to Elbasan. He was sheltered by the Nosi family and worked as a chemist in a factory owned by them. Marko had false papers and was living as a Moslem, but at a wedding a German recognized him as a Jew and he was arrested by the Gestapo.

Vasil Nosi knew a high ranking German officer from his school days in Austria. The German was an alcoholic and was kept well supplied by Vasil. The German got Marko out of jail "just this one time" and brought him to the Nosi home.

Marko was moved to the village of Lixhat where he was kept in hiding in an abandoned hotel until liberation. During that time he saw only Adelina Nosi, who brought him food.

After the war, Marko had a visa and was ready to go to Israel, but the Communists had arrested Vasil Nosi. Marko and Vasil's brother tried to get him released and in turn they were arrested and imprisoned. Vasil died in prison and Marko spent four years in a Communist prison for interfering and trying to help a friend.

When Marko got out of prison his exit visa had expired and the Hoxha Government opposed emigration to Israel

so he was trapped. His move to Israel was delayed until 1991, 45 years after his first attempt.

The members of the Nosi family have been honored as Righteous Gentiles.

Beqir Qoqja
Beqir's Jewish friend, Avraham Eliasaf (who used the Moslem name of Gani) was living in Beqir's tailor shop in Tirana. When the Germans made a "sweep" looking for Jews they agreed it was safer to move Avraham to a remote village where he would "pass" as a Moslem. Avraham had some gold coins that he gave Beqir for helping him. After liberation Beqir returned the gold coins to his friend and refused all compensation, and took offense at the suggestion that he take the gold coins.

Beqir visited Israel with the group of Righteous, but they didn't have their planed reunion, Avraham died just before the visit.

Beqir has been designated as a Righteous gentile.

This wasn't an isolated case where property was returned after the war. Nadire Buxhiu turned back to the Jews all the valuables they had left in trust with her. Haim David left some art objects of great value with his friend Hazhi Mulla Delliu. Haim didn't survive, so Hazhi turned the objects over to Haim's daughter even though she probably had no knowledge of the objects. In a similar instance Mrs. Qirko gave to Samuel Matathia's sons all the valuables their father had left with her.

The Prefect of Vlora, an important figure in the days of the Italian occupation was picking up some merchandise his wife selected at Pepe Levi's store. Pepe told the Prefect he must not trouble himself and could pay the bill when he liked; meaning never. The Prefect had the power to arrest all Jews and confiscate all their goods. As a practical matter he could have taken anything he wanted. He got

irritated at Levi's suggestion and answered, "Listen to me Pepe Levi. I have been a friend of yours and have expressed myself as your friend. If you think I have done that to profit anything you are wrong. Now give me the bill otherwise I will consider you an enemy."

Metin, Azis and Shpresa Ruli – Ali Kuci
Shpresa Ruli and her parents Metin & Azis and Ali Kuci became friends with Solomon Konforti and his wife and new born daughter. Ali provided false papers and the Ruli-Kuci family took the Konfortis under their "protection." During a period of seven months they kept moving the Konfortis from place to place where Ruli could protect them.

One day Solomon, for unexplained reasons, went into town and was promptly arrested. The Jewish family had documents that identified them as Moslems. Using personal contacts the Moslem family was able to get Solomon released claiming he was Ali's brother. It was too dangerous to stay in Tirana so they were taken to a small town. In September, 1944, the Komforti family got to Milan, and safety, and in January, 1945, they returned to Yugoslavia and then to Israel. The families still correspond 50 years later.

Ali was a known anti-Communist and was tortured and killed by the Communists in 1945. The son of Ali came with the group to Israel representing the Ruli and Kuci families.

The Budo Family
Their daughter, Sado Xhyheri, hid four Jewish men: Riketa Goni, Viktor Jakoel, Eftimi Jakoel, and David Matathia. Sado would spend most of each day with the Jews keeping them company and encouraging them to keep up their spirits. This good relation has continued through the years.

The Battino family stayed hidden in the Budo home in Tirana for 40 days. After the Germans bombed the town it

became risky so they were moved to a small town where they would be safer. It was not unusual for Jews to be passed from one rescuer to another resulting in more than one person or family being accredited as Righteous for rescuing a single Jew or Jewish family.

Besim and Aishe Kadiu

During the spring and summer 1944, during the most dangerous time, the Kadiu family opened their door and sheltered a Jewish family.

Shyqyri Myrto

Shyqyri was a very good friend of Josef Jakoel. In March, 1944, during a "control" by Kosovars working for the Germans, an effort was made to collect all identity cards from Jews. The next step would be deportation. Shyqyri hid Josef Jakoel and his sister Eriketa from March until November, 1944.

One night the Germans came. They may have had information that Shyqyri was hiding Jews. The door wasn't opened until Josef was far away. Eriketa was dressed in characteristic clothes of the central part of the country, and was hidden in the woman's room where males were forbidden to enter. The Germans were persuaded not to enter as they were told a man could not enter the woman's room under any circumstances.

Fifty years later, sitting in a comfortable home in Israel, Shyqyri, and his friend Beqir Qoqja, were asked about these events of so many years ago. Shyqyri, now age 80, wearing an old beret and leaning on his cane, listened while Josef Jakoel's daughter told the story of the rescue of her father: "When the raid was over he led my father and his sister from house to house, from yard to yard, under the nose of the Germans who were hunting for Jews, until he brought them to a safe place in the country." Her eyes were full of admiration for the man who saved her father and aunt from almost certain death.

We asked these two old Moslem men why they did these noble acts. Beqir, a farmer who isn't used to speaking very much, simply said, "He is my friend." Shyqyri interjected, "Maybe you call this humanism. Our Moslem religion says we must help someone who is in danger in difficult times." Beqir disagreed, "This has nothing to do with religion. We all have one God and he has commanded us to help others. It's the same thing Jesus said, that Muhammad has commanded, and actually your Moses said the same thing."

Other Righteous Gentiles
Over 80 fugitive Jews, mostly unknown to her, passed through the home of Nadire Bixhiu who found places of safety for them. Hoxha Ferri guided many Jews to the village of Zall-Herr, where he had a spacious house. There was a big crowd and they fed 80 people from this house, including some Italian soldiers who escaped from the army when Italy surrendered.

The Solomon family and others were hidden in the house of Nuro Hoxha, in Vlora. As a precaution a trench was created that could hold all 17 of Huxha's "guests." The 17 stayed in this house for three months.

In 1940, Vjera Matusevic and her family of 7 were living in Tirana when the Germans came. They were moved to Zall-Herr where food was provided for them by Mikel Kilica. The Germans learned about what Mikel was doing so he moved them to the Monastery of Ardenica where the Bishop provided the Jews with false papers. They were discovered and moved back to Tirana, to the house of Vasil Bidoshi, where they stayed until liberation.

Some of the refugees were sent to Berat by the Albanian authorities. It was their good fortune because the people of Berat, such as Abdullah Shkodrani, Xhevdet Gjiergjani, and others, kept them hidden and fed them.

Toli Todi, from Kavaja, sheltered Joseph Adixhes. The Gjata brothers, from Fier, hid Mosha Basar.

Abdullah Shkodrani gave shelter to Rashel David, and in Shkodra, Xhevat Bekteshi saved Jashar Barukovic.

In February, 1942, the Germans ordered Albanian officials to arrest and turn over to them all Jews who had illegally crossed the border from Serbia. The mayors were asked to provide information as to fugitives living in their towns. The mayors responded that there were no Jews in their towns, although, in reality, there were dozens of them.

The beginning of 1944 was not the start of a good year. On the first day of the year the Germans arrested a group of citizens of Vlora. They came in the middle of night and arrested individuals in accordance with a list they carried. All those arrested were taken to concentration camps. Some were shot in the city of Resnia in Yugoslavia. There were 700 people arrested that night and only a few returned. There were no Jews among the 700. They had taken one Jew but someone intervened for him and he was freed. The methodical Nazis were saving the Jews for a special "round up."

On another day in February, the Nazis killed 90 people shooting them in their homes and on the street. The Nazis did a house to house search for Jews and collected their papers and ordered them to report to the SS office in two days. The Jews knew if they entered that place they would never come out alive. Friends provided them with false names and documents.

Not every story can be told in detail, and there were many rescues that have not yet been recognized. For example, the wife of Fatlli Imami, Irena, of Slav origin, hid Jewish friends she knew from before the war. The number of Jews wanting hiding places was increasing and there came a time when her small house was filled. Fatlli and his wife didn't want to refuse anybody so they enlisted the help of other Albanian families in hiding Jews.

56

The Jews were spread over many cities and villages in Albania, such as Lushnja, Shijak, Kavaja, Berat, Fier, and Kruja. Some Jews were helped by friends with whom they had a long relation before the war. Others were helped by people they didn't know until they opened their door.

Although the Jews of Albania survived they still had deep loses. Most had relatives in Janina and Corfu where very few escaped. There were 28 members of Zhaneta Solomon's family and only 2 survived. Jakoel lost his 25 year old sister with her 2 year old daughter and 5 year old son. His sister had married a man from Corfu where they made their home. There were few survivors on Corfu.

Chapter Nine

Survivors Tell Their Stories

Johanna Jutta Neumann
My parents and I came from Germany to Albania in 1939. We were grateful to obtain Albanian visas. We came by way of Italy and sailed overnight to Durrës. We found some 60 other emigrants in Durrës and Tirana. Three weeks later Italy invaded Albania.

In September, 1940, we, together with other emigrants, evacuated to Berat, where we rented a room. At that time we had very little money, receiving only a small stipend from the Albanian Government. The Moslem family that rented us the room helped us greatly, especially with food. The friendship and hospitality they showed us was a wonderful experience.

The British bombed Berat daily so we got permission to move to Lushnja and stayed there until June, 1941. My father was an amateur painter and he made a living painting pictures and signs for stores.

In the summer of 1941, we were given permission to move back to Durrës, and we rented a room from a farmer in Shkozet. In February, 1942, two Italian soldiers tried to break into our apartment. The owner broke though a wall so we could escape through his home if it should become necessary.

An Albanian policeman recognized my parents and had them arrested. Ing Pilku, and his wife Charlotte, who were our first landlords and friends, were able to arrange my parents release after a few days.

When the Germans arrived, in 1943, we went into hiding. My father, who was easily identifiable as a Jew, went to Kruja. My mother and I moved into the Pilku home and claimed to be members of Charolette's German family.

It wasn't until the late summer of 1944 before the Germans found us and took us to SS headquarters to register us. We were lucky the Germans were tied down fighting partisans and didn't have time for us. By November the Germans were forced out of Albania and we were free. We survived due to the courage, friendship, and hospitality of the Albanian people. We left Albania in September, 1945.

Statement of Dr. Anna Kohen

My family was from Janina (less than 10% of the Jewish community survived). We went into the mountains near Vlora, changed our names for Moslem ones, and blended perfectly with the Moslems who treated us like their own brothers and sisters.

Irene Grunbaum

In a recent book relating her experiences as a Jew in wartime Albania, Irene Grunbaum pays homage to the people of Albania. After describing her experiences, in her final paragraph about Albania she wrote:

> "Farewell Albania, I thought. You have given me so much, hospitality, refuge, friends, and adventures. Farewell Albania, one day I will tell the world how brave, fearless, strong and faithful your sons are, how death and the devil can't frighten them. If necessary I'll tell how they protected a refugee and wouldn't allow her to be harmed even if it meant losing their lives. The gates of your small country remained open, Albania. Your authorities closed both eyes, when necessary, to give poor persecuted people another chance to survive the most horrible of all wars. Albania, we survived the siege because of your humanity. We thank you."[1]

Others have echoed Mrs. Grunbaum's sentiments. Soon after the war ended the Jewish community of Yugoslavia praised and thanked the Albanian people for their humanity. A Jewish engineer broadcast a radio message of gratitude to the people of Albania. He is quoted as having said, "The Albanian, owing to his very liberal nature, has always judged a man on the basis of his personal merits and was merciful to the oppressed and to refugees."

He continued, "All Jews who were forced to leave Yugoslavia owing to German rule found a liberal home and generous people in Albania."

"Why?"
How can we account for the survival of the Jewish community of Albania, including the foreign Jews who were fortunate enough to get within its protective borders? Why did the Albanians take the risk of sheltering Jews? The moral code of the Albanians "the Kanun" plus the concept of the "Besa" must be the answer.

Yet there are other possible answers and the truth may be found in one, all or in a combination of the answers.

The Jews of Albania were Albanians, this requires further elucidation. The Jews of Albania were members of the community, few spoke Yiddish or Ladino. They spoke Albanian and some Greek, as did their neighbors. They did not set themselves apart from other Albanians, although they tended to live in small Jewish neighborhoods.

The Jews were educated professionals and tradesmen in disproportion to their numbers, but they were not so numerous that they overwhelmed the others as contrasted to some other countries where there were professions and trades where Jews were in the majority.

We can compare the relation of the Albanian Jews to other Albanians, to the relation of the Jews of Salonika, to the other Salonikans. The Holocaust took the lives of more

than 90% of the Jews of Salonika. That a few Jews of that city survived is attributed almost totally to Righteous Greeks, who risked their lives to save friends or business friends. The extremes of 100% being rescued in one place and less than 10% in another is worthy of a separate research project.

It's accepted that the smaller the number of Jews in the community the greater the likelihood of the Jews being accepted and befriended. In wartime Albania, the Jewish population swelled by at least 800 and possibly as many as 1,000. The Jews still constituted less than 1% of the population. In Salonika, Jews constituted somewhere between 30% and 40% of the population. Their prosperity was evident on a daily basis, which couldn't be a positive factor. One of the great differences was that the Jews of Salonika, even today, speak a language of their own, Ladino, which doesn't endear them to other Salonikian. They were not Salokians in the sense that Albanian Jews were Albanians.

At first glance, a better study would be to compare the experience of the Jews of Janina to the Albanians. To date, no one has been designated a Righteous Gentile in Janina but that's not a good or fair test because the Germans rounded up the Jews in a single day, which didn't permit them, or their friends, the time to falsify documents, establish hiding places, or take any action to escape. The rapidity with which the Germans organized their action in Janina suggests that the Germans had a list of Jews. Who provided this list, if in fact there was such a list? Was it the civil authority as it seems to have been in the annexed territories? Or was it the Jewish community itself as it was in Salonika?

The policy of the Albanian Government, including the puppet governments put into power by the Italians and the Germans, was to protect Albanians and the Jews were Albanians.

The Regency created by the Germans refused to supply lists or to collect Jews in a single location. They treated this as an infringement of their right to govern the internal affairs of their country. We can only speculate on why the Germans accepted this response, but they did. This was very important but doesn't answer the question as it relates to foreign Jews.

The distinction between Albania and other countries concerning protecting foreigners is of great significance. For example, the French and Bulgarian Governments cooperated with the Nazis demands for arresting foreign Jews, but refused to turn their own nationals over to the Germans, although France eventually did this.

The good relations, the small numbers, etc. go towards answering the question of why there was little or no anti-Semitism in Albania, but it doesn't answer the question of why the Albanians were willing to risk their lives to rescue Jews. Even if we debate the question of the extent of the risk there was the cost and inconvenience of hiding the Jews. This is especially important when we consider that oftentimes the rescuers didn't know the Jews before they took them into their home, and often times they didn't have a common language.

This brings us back to the moral code of the Albanians which governs day to day life. This code is a way of life in Albania and differs from other codes to which people give lip service but ignore in practice. The attitude towards refugees was a life saver for the foreign Jews who sought refuge in Albania. The concept of the responsibility of a guest in one's home was considered to include a guest-refuge in one's country.

In some other countries, a distinction was made between protecting foreign Jews and native Jews. No such distinction was made in Albania, all Jews were protected. Even those Albanians who cooperated with the Germans, for one reason or another, did not violate the code of honor as it related to the Jews in Albania.

The Moral Code of Albanians

"There are no foreigners in Albania, there are only guests. Our moral code as Albanians requires that we be hospitable to guests in our home and in our country," according to Refik Veseli. When asked about the possibility of Albanians reporting the presence of the Jews to the Germans, he said it was possible, but if an Albanian did this he would have disgraced his village and his family. At a minimum his home would be destroyed and his family banished. This discussion was pointless as "no Albanian disgraced us."

The moral code of the Albanian people distinguishes them from other peoples of Europe. This small group who lived under harsh economic conditions emerged as the most moral society of the ugly days of World War II.

It was amongst the mountain people that the moral code arose which governs the Albanians. In passing years, this was collected in a Book of Laws, known as the Kanun. According to Antonia Young,[2] scholars believe that the Kanun could be the basis for an entire legal system. The Kanun is traditional in North Albania, and other versions of the code exist in other parts of the country. Hoxha tried to outlaw the code, but even this dictator couldn't wipe it out.

The code is also known as the Code of Dukagjini, named for a 15th century chieftain who standardized the oral codes. The code wasn't reduced to writing until a Roman Catholic priest tried to do this in 1913. He was murdered for his efforts, but other priests carried on and in 1933 the 1262 articles of the code were first published. The code applies equally to Moslem and Christians.

Following are some of the most important articles of the Kanun affecting the Jews who received refuge in Albania.

"The Albanian home is at the service of God and the sojourner."

It's of interest that the word sojourner is used instead of traveler, as it suggests a length of stay rather than a short respite. It is a greater burden to house and protect a sojourner than a traveler.

"Every hour of the day and night, a man must be ready to receive a guest with bread, salt, and an open heart. He must offer him a bed, a pillow, and a warm hearth."

To the delight of the Jewish refugees seeking shelter from the Nazi killing machine, "guest" meant guests in the country as well as guests in home.

"Every man can see himself as a good man when he is addressed as a man of honor."

Giving shelter to a sojourner is a heavy responsibility, especially if he is in danger of his life. If one fails in this responsibility, according to the Kanun, your name and your honor is ruined forever. The word for preserving your honor is BESA. "The Albanian must honor his Besa."

According to Hamdi Mecaj, "Besa means simply this; if an Albanian gives his word he will kill his own son rather than break it. That's all! Besa is forever. If an Albanian gave you his Besa and does not fulfill it or cheats you, his honor is lost!" When he said this he slide one hand across the other as he said "That's all." In an earlier meeting with Jakoel he made an identical gesture as he said the very same words.

"If an Albanian is treacherous to those who trusted him - his community has a duty to destroy him and no vengeance may be sought for his blood."

"All are equal before God. The handsome and the ugly are of equal importance."

"A man must defend his guest's honor even if he endangers his own life in doing so."

This article makes one think of Refik Veseli standing in the doorway letting no German pass except over his dead body. It also reminds us of Mihal going to the police station to steal blank identity cards for distribution to the refugees.

This is only a small portion of the Kanun, but it answers the question of Why.

Footnotes:
1. Escape Through the Balkans, p.139.
    "Reprinted from *Escape Through The Balkans: The Autobiography of Irene Grunbaum*. Translated and edited with an introduction by Katherine Morris by permission of the University of Nebraska Press.© 1996 by Katherine Morris."
2. Deciphering the 'Code' Illria February 1, 1995, p.6.

Chapter Ten

After World War II

On November 8, 1941, in reaction to fascist ideology, the Albanian Communist party was formed with Enver Hoxha as its head. No one could have predicted in that year the negative influence which this one man would have on their lives for the next 50 years.

At the end of 1944, Albanians celebrated their short lived freedom. Enver Hoxha, the leader of the Albanian partisans, declared Albania a Communist state and named himself the absolute dictator. He didn't hesitate to murder or jail his opponents and used the scare technique, relying on the Albanian fear of foreign invasion, as the justification for having a strong dictator.

Anyone visiting Albania today can't escape seeing the "pill boxes" or "bunkers" pointing in every direction. Some reports say there are 30,000 and others say 60,000 of these concrete bunkers. They are to defend Albania from foreign invaders. Bunkers are everywhere.

In Hoxha's day every able bodied citizen was assigned to a bunker. Who were they defending against? The United States, of course.

The bunkers are deserted now and there is no practical way to dispose of these giant poured concrete mushrooms.

Gradually, Hoxha severed Albanian contacts with other countries, and in 1961, he broke with the Soviet Union when he made an alliance with Communist China. When China opened to the West, Hoxha saw this as treachery, and that unusual alliance was ended. That was Albania's last contact with the outside world which Hoxha

considered evil. Contact with Albania became impossible, and Albanians discouraged foreign friends from sending letters, lest this lead to police inquires.

Incredibly, Hoxha decided that the Soviet Union and other countries, which formerly had Socialist systems, had degenerated into Capitalist systems.

In 1985, Hoxha died after being the European leader who ruled for the longest duration after the World War. His casket was followed by thousands of people. Others hid their joy. Those who "mourned" him didn't feel free enough to destroy his monument until five years later.

In 1990, Hoxha's successor, Ramiz Alia, succumbed to public pressure and declared free elections. The same year telephone links to the west were opened. In 1991, the Democratic Party won the elections, and the ravages of the Hoxha regime became apparent.

Poverty in Albania was everywhere. The average salary was $20.00 a month, and a loaf of bread cost 50 cents. Shops and gas stations were guarded by iron bars, and unemployment was rampant. Huge industrial projects failed and factories lay idle. Albania could not compete in world markets.

In 1969, all income and sales taxes were abolished and this is formalized in the 1976 constitution. The state receives its income from enterprises and foreign trade. Recently an income tax was imposed.

The Jews After the War
The Jewish population quickly shrank even before the war ended. The refugees returned home as one country after another was liberated. Only then did they learn of the full horror of the Holocaust. Many left to seek entry to what was to become Israel. Few stayed to become Albanian citizens, and most of those who stayed did so because they had married Albanians.

67

A Polish Jewish woman who married an Albanian rejected the offer of help to get her to Israel as a new emigrant even though her husband died. She has chosen to remain in Albania "to be with my friends."

It has been estimated that after the World War there were only 85 Jewish families living in Albania. That figure seems rather low. When the war ended there were 600 Jews in Albania, according to Jakoel. Others estimate there were as many as 1,000. From 1933 until 1945 there were Jews entering and moving out of Albania, and it's impossible to know their number; 500, 1000, 3000? It's only for the period of the German occupation, the late summer, 1943, until November, 1944, that the Jewish population was stable (and in hiding). The best estimate for this period is 800-1000 native and foreign Jews were in hiding.

Under the Communists
After the war, Albanians lived in a police state that limited the freedom of all Albanians, Jews were not singled out for special treatment. It was dangerous to speak a foreign language, read certain books, express certain opinions, listen to foreign radio or watch foreign television.

Josef Jakoel listened to Voice of America, the BBC, and the Greek and Italian radio, taking the risk of arrest, in order to find out what was happening in the rest of the world.

Jakoel's father owned a small factory and was arrested and stayed in jail until all his properties were turned over to the Communists. After he gave up everything he owned, he was freed and was allowed a very small house.

Israel
In 1949, an unsuccessful effort was made by some Jews to go to Israel. This was strictly forbidden and the Jews were forced to remain in Tirana and Vlora, where most of the Jews lived after the Second World War. In 1953, some Jews were killed trying to escape to Italy. Other Jews escaped into Greece and it was estimated that there were 52

Albanian Jewish families living in Greece at this time. [1] It was a period of terror, according to Izack Cohen, one of the leaders of the Jewish community.

According to the Encyclopedia Judaica, there were about 200 Jews living in Tirana in 1969, and also some in Vlora and Shkodra, but the Jews in Tirana were mostly Sephardim. Jakoel said that the last part of the statement is in error.

The Albanian Government, following the lead of the Russians in the United Nations voted in favor of statehood for Israel. When the Soviets switched to an anti-Israel position the Albanian puppets followed and remained anti-Israel. The Albanian Government wanted to show continued support for the Palestinians and took a long term anti-Israel posture, which created an uncomfortable situation for Jews. It didn't help that Israel supported Albania's resolution to bring Communist China into the United Nations.

Albania established diplomatic relations with Israel on August 19, 1991. There are favorable signs that there will be good relations between the two countries. The Albanian Government didn't stand in the way of the Jewish exodus in 1991.

In 1995, the Kibbutz Orchestra of Israel, the Chorus of the Opera Theater of Tirana, and some members of the Opera Orchestra of Tirana, joined together to perform a concert in honor of the Albanian Righteous. Things are looking up.

There is disagreement as to whether there was anti-Semitism in postwar Albania. There were instances of taunts by children who had learned about Albanian opposition to Israel, as was common in Communist countries. A Jewish woman felt that it was anti-Semitism when she was not allowed to study at the Conservatory of Music, as she was highly qualified. Another Jewish woman bases her statement that there was no discrimination on

the fact that so many Albanian Jews are professionals and have advanced degrees. There was also the possibility that the denial of entry into the Conservatory of Music was attributed to the fact that this woman had a wealthy grandfather, which was a crime for citizens of Communist Albania.

In 1986, the Jewish chronicle reported that a Jew who "escaped" from Albania by crossing the mountains from Albania to Greece claimed that anti-Semitism was rife in Albania. Many Albanian Jews disagree.

The Atheistic State
It would be easy, but a mistake, to conclude that the lack of intense religion in Albania is due solely to the Hoxha Government's outlawing of religion. In a history of Albania written in 1919, a generation before Hoxha, there is a comment that Albanians historically have been indifferent to religion. King Zog had terminated relations with Moslems outside Albania in the 1930s. Toleration of other religions exists here like no where else.

One reason for this unique situation may be the fact there has been relatively little conversion "by the sword." The Turks were certainly Moslems and welcomed conversions, but rarely put the issue before the people as "convert or die." At most, conversions to Islam were for personal gain, convenience, or influence, and not religious zeal. Living in a Moslem country it was often expedient to be a Moslem. The Turks knew this and so did the neighbors and the people who converted. It is understandable that under these circumstances relatively few people took religion seriously.

Like the Jews of Spain, who were Christians by day and Jews at night, the new converts to Islam often did the same, but there was one important difference. In Spain it was often fatal if a "Christian" was found to be a secret Jew or Moslem, but in Albania no one seemed to care if a new Moslem followed Christian practices in his home.

70

Heavy intermarriage often resulted in a conversion to Islam. Here again expediency was a major factor. Having multi-religion families also contributed towards toleration. It was not uncommon for brothers to have different religions. It was also common for Christians to give their children nice-sounding Moslem names.

There were also conversions of Christians back and forth between the Roman Catholic and Orthodox religions based on economic or political considerations. The national hero is known to have converted and his father is reputed to have made more than one conversion.

Jews converted, but how many and how often is unknown. In 1936, Herman Bernstein wrote that Moslem clergy in Albania told him that it was very likely their ancestors were Jews.

One Moslem cleric told Bernstein, it was likely that his entire village were Jews at one time. He based this, in large part, on the Jewish sounding names which were common in his village. Did this attitude have any baring on the sensitivity of Albanians to the plight of the foreign and domestic Jews during the Holocaust years?

The Atheistic Society was imposed in 1967 by the Communist Government. Until that year there was religious toleration and the people were free to exercise their religious beliefs and customs. Albania has the distinction of being the world's first totally atheistic state. The laws and the anti-religion restrictions placed on the populous were much more detailed and restrictive than the laws in the Soviet Union and the Soviet bloc countries.

Hoxha's assertion was that the religion of Albanians was "Albaniaism." The reason or excuse for the abolition of religion was to make the country homogeneous and to reduce outside influence. It was almost a quarter of a century before the anti-religion laws were repealed or safely ignored.

Starting in 1967, the Government carried out a campaign against religion which resulted in the closing of all churches and Mosques. This was not done without bloodshed as there was anti-religion violence. For example, there was a report that four Franciscan monks were burned to death in a Roman Catholic church and convent.

The anti-religion campaign included the destruction or burning of religious books and the punishment of anyone who dared to act contrary to the anti-religion law. The clerics of the three major religions were made civil service workers and were soon pensioned off. Mosques and churches were closed and some were made into museums. For a time old people were allowed to practice their religion at home, but this soon ended.

There were no anti-Semitic overtones to the abolition of religion as the restrictions applied to all religions. In the same vein the Jews were not exempt from this law, but as will be seen, some Jews (and others) often violated the law. One violation was that the Jakoels often had religious gatherings, that ended when the 1976 Albania constitution was adopted which contained a specific provision forbidding religious gatherings.

The Jakoel family engaged in a number of illegal practices, including the translation into the Albanian language of information about Israel, Jewish history, and Jewish traditions. These materials were circulated throughout the Jewish community in Albania. "An article or book about Israel was like a feast for us," was Jakoel's comment.

In 1967, all places of worship were closed, religious books were banned, religious rites and ceremonies were prohibited, and putting a religious designation on a tombstone was a criminal offense.

Although the atheistic society started in 1967 its full impact wasn't felt until 1975 when the most oppressive period started. Jewish identity deteriorated starting in

1975 and there was no contact with Jews from "outside" with the exception of some visiting Russian doctors.

In 1988, there were the first signs of the loosening of the restrictions on religion when emigre religious leaders were permitted limited visits. In November, 1990, a Roman Catholic priest, recently released after 26 years in prison, conducted a service for Christians and Moslems. He was arrested, but was soon freed after public demonstrations on his behalf.

By the end of December, 1990, most restrictions on religion were lifted and the law against the public practice of religion was rescinded. The mosques and churches were opened two months later.

Once the dictatorship ended, the people, mostly the older folks, opened old churches and built a few new churches, but there are many new masques. Outside some of the new masques are pictorial signs explaining the proper positions and methods of prayer. There is a generation that knows very little about its own religion.

The religious breakdown, according to the best information available, is Moslem 70%, Orthodox 20% and Roman Catholic 10%. The Jewish percentage during the 20th century has never been more than a small fraction of 1%.

Jewish Life Before And During the Atheistic Period
The "Beyond" part of this discussion is short when we consider that the end of the atheistic period (1990) is almost concurrent with the major Jewish exodus to Israel.

Burial
Until 1967 Jews were buried in a corner, or section, of Moslem cemeteries as a gesture of good will from the Moslem community. There was one exception, an ancient Jewish cemetery in Vlora, reportedly dating back to the 9th century, was used until 1965.

After the imposition of the atheistic state all burials were in civic cemeteries without separation or identification by religion. In 1967, the old cemeteries were destroyed by the Government and the tombstones were moved to the new cemeteries. The Government also permitted the transfer of remains. In the process, Jewish headstones were found dating from the 9th century onward.

Until 1967 funerals were performed with great pedantism and strictly followed Jewish law. The body was washed and wrapped in white linen and laid in a coffin, but burial was without the coffin. The body was taken to the cemetery accompanied by mourners singing the funeral prayers along the way.

Mourning lasted 40 days, and during the first 8 days the family slept on the ground and ate in a leaning position. The men didn't shave for 40 days, and every night during this period a minyon (group of 10 or more men) gathered to say the prayer for the dead.

Rabbis
The presence of rabbis in the early middle ages is verified by the writing of the much traveled Rabbi Benjamin of Tudela, who visited Albania in 1170, and refers to Rabbi's Soloman and Jacob living in the area.

There were resident rabbis during the early years, but the 20th century Jewish community was never large enough to support a full time rabbi. Community members would act as "hazen," following the tradition of Turkish Jews who combine rabbi and cantor in one person.

For decades the Jewish community in Albania relied on rabbis from Corfu to bless marriages and sometimes officiate at circumcisions. After the Holocaust there is no Jewish community in Corfu and after 1967 no rabbi was permitted to visit Albania. Every religious practice was forbidden.

Circumcision
The Jewish community has no moel to perform the circumcision and relied on Moslems who willingly performed this function. Moslems follow the practice of circumcision which was continued past 1967, but in secret. Before the war it was common to have the moel come from Corfu to perform the circumcision but this ended with the war.

Normally the circumcision is done 8 days after birth, but in 20th century Albania it was done later. The last ritual circumcision were during the Italian occupation, they continued in secret, but without the religious ceremony. The Moslem doing the circumcision was usually a barber with special training. It is evident that the circumcision were not done according to Jewish law, but the important fact is that it was done.

Synagogues
There hasn't been a synagogue in Albania since the last one was accidentally destroyed during the First World War. The make shift synagogues were in the homes of those Jews who had large houses who were willing to use a portion of their home in this manner. The Jakoel family used two rooms that converted into one large room for this purpose and this helped establish them as leaders of the community. After 1975 it became too risky to conduct religious gatherings.

Marriage
Like most Jewish communities there was a strong preference that children marry within the faith. Before the Second World War to marry outside the faith was scandalous. There were two incidents in 1935 of Jewish girls marrying Christians. The parents and community felt these marriages were a damnation. Their families were disgraced and one family went so far as to recite the prayer for the dead, disowning their erring daughter. Things change rapidly and it's estimated that as many as 50% of the post 1967 marriages have been to non-Jews.

The prewar marriages were mostly to the Jews of Janina. There were relatively few marriages to the Jews of Corfu because they spoke a Venetian dialect that was unknown to many Jews of Albania. An eligible son or daughter would go to Janina to visit cousins, to work or go to school until he or she met the right person.

There were some marriages within the Albanian Jewish community and they often were between spouses that had known each other since childhood. The "pool" of prospective mates wasn't very large, but the children knew this from an early age and they knew what was expected of them. To many Jews marriage outside the faith is still unthinkable.

All this changed in the years after the Second World War and especially the years after 1967. There no longer is a pool of prospective mates in Corfu or Janina. Finding a suitable mate had always been a problem, but the situation worsened as the traditional trips abroad to visit cousins were no longer possible, and the pool in Albania was small.

The choices were reduced to three. There were the lucky ones who were able to find an acceptable Jewish mate from among what was available. Some were so anxious to marry within the faith that they were willing to make a selection that might not otherwise have been acceptable. For the parents this was the best possible choice. There were no arranged marriages, but the families couldn't help but push children of marriageable age together.

The second choice was to remain unmarried. This is against Jewish tradition, and it is readily apparent that few chose this option. The third option was to marry a non-Jew.

No statistics have been seen, but there is a definite possibility that as many as 50% of the marriages since 1967 have been to non-Jewish partners. What had been

scandalous has become common place. Parents understood the problem facing their children yet they still wanted their children to marry within the faith. The evidence of this is that one of the most common reasons given for emigrating to Israel is to have the children marry Jews.

Courting wasn't too dissimilar from the rest of Europe, e.g. a stroll in the park, a movie, a concert, a meal, visiting married friends, etc. There was one major difference, the assumption placed on the "appearance" of female virginity.

This presented a problem for the modern woman. After an unspecified number of dates with one individual the assumption is that they have been intimate. It's a clash between the puritanical prewar attitudes versus the postwar opportunities. Whether the assumption of intimacy was valid or not, the young woman became damaged if she dated one person too many times. Her chances of a good marriage within the Jewish community, which were small at best, disappeared. With the size of the Jewish community being what it was, there was little that escaped notice.

This placed an additional burden on the young woman. After a relatively few dates she had to make a decision. If the relation continued, but didn't result in marriage, she risked ever finding a suitable spouse. If she prematurely terminated the relation she may have given up her only chance at a good marriage. The double standard prevailed at its worst.

Weddings took place at the homes big enough to hold the ceremony and the wedding feast. It was a great honor for the owner of a big house to be asked to make it available for a wedding. The marriage ceremony was usually conducted in accordance with strict Jewish law until 1967. The couple was covered with a talise (prayer shawl) and drank the ritual wine from the same cup which was then

smash as a reminder of the destruction of King Soloman's Temple. A contract of marriage was then prepared in Hebrew and given to the bride's parents.

Prior to 1967, religious wedding ceremonies were permitted if preceded by a civil ceremony. In 1967, and thereafter, there were only civil ceremonies. There were a few secret religious weddings, but in Jakoel's opinion the risk was too great.

The Israeli Government has taken a realistic and a practical approach to the fact that there were many non-Jews in the group of Albanian emigrants. The non-Jewish spouse and the child or grandchild of a Jew have been given the same rights, including the right to some financial support as is provided to any Jewish emigrant.

In these inter-religious marriages it seems that overwhelmingly they go in the direction of Judaism with the Jewish spouse remaining a Jew and the children being raised as Jews. This may be because the Jewish partner has more knowledge and education about his religion than does the non-Jewish partner. The Moslem or Christian partner wasn't faced with the limited pool so this person wasn't likely to be concerned with his own religion or he would not have married a Jew.

There was no preference for marriage to a Moslem versus a Christian. The fact the majority of these marriages were with Moslems may be a reflection of the fact that there were 7 Moslems to every 3 Christians, and most Christians lived in the north and the Jews lived in the central and southern parts of the country.

Kosher
Kosher food was not available so non-kosher meat was eaten by most Jews. A few became vegetarians because of the absence of kosher meat. Jews refrained from eating pork and other foods prohibited by Jewish law.

Holidays
Before the atheistic period the shops of Jewish merchants would be closed during the Jewish holidays. After 1967 the Jewish owned shops would have to stay open and the children would go to school and the parents would go to work on Yom Kippour and Rosh Hashona. However, acting as inconspicuous as possible the Jews would fast without calling attention to themselves.

The supper before Yom Kippur, a day of fasting, was always a great joy. Almost all the men would spend the day in prayer in a room lit by candles with olive oil sent by every family to the home where the prayer gathering was held. After the holiday ended at night one by one the congregates used to leave holding a lighted candle. The light parade continued onto the street, fading slowly until it disappeared, this practice ended in 1967.

Passover matzos were baked at home because no real matzo were available. It was a beautiful day in the spring of 1945 when the Jews received 1,500 pounds of matzo flour from the Janina Relief Agency.

Jakoel's daughter recalls, "I remember the excitement would build for Passover. Our grandfather would read the Hagadah in Hebrew, he was educated at a Jewish religious school in Greece. I also remember the unique way we learned Bible studies. It was prohibited to own a Bible. Parents would seemingly make up fairy tales to tell their children and present them as such, but anyone who knew the Bible recognized these stories."

Purim was the favorite holiday because there were no deprivations. On Purim, Jews would give gifts to each other. The best food was served on this holiday, and small coins would be given to the children who would wear masks and go from door to door asking their friends and relatives if they recognized them.

Hanukkah lasted for 8 days and the candles were lit for all 8 days. During the feasts of the holidays there were visits from family and non-Jewish friends. Like the ancient Hebrews they often weren't sure of the dates of holidays so they would listen to an Italian radio station hoping to get hints as to when a holiday started.

Hebrew Language
Few Albanian Jews knew Hebrew before going to Israel, and the Hebrew they knew was for prayers and not conversational Hebrew. In most countries potential emigrants to Israel start to study Hebrew in advance of their immigration, but the Albanians did not have this opportunity as they came from a country where studying the Hebrew language was a criminal offense

Jewish Homes
There is a Jewish woman living in Vlora married to a Moslem, who identifies as a Jew and has raised her two sons as Jews. She elected not to join her father who moved to Israel in 1991. Her family home in Vlora is a big house which had been confiscated by the Communists and in recent years was used as a public library. In 1994, the state was in the process of restoring the house to her family, with the delay being caused by the difficulty in finding a new home for the library.

There is a small unpainted space on the door frame where it was obvious a mizor had been. She said that before her time the big room in the house had been used as a synagogue.

The house next door, also a very big house, had belonged to the Jacob Levy family and is now the offices of the National Democratic Party. The next house in the row had also belonged the Levy family. These three houses were mansions and are far superior to typical Albanian homes and far, far, superior to the homes on Jew Street.

The official name for the street was Jew Street and this was not a pejorative, it is descriptive. Many Jewish families had lived on this one block long street. The houses on Jew Street were very modest, even by Albanian standards. The street and its name are well known and it served to demonstrate that not all Jews in Vlora lived in mansions. Jakoel had lived on this street until his family moved to Tirana, in 1950.

No Jews live on this Jew Street today but the name remains. At no time was this a ghetto as the Jews lived here voluntarily and there were always some gentile families living on the street. The last Jewish family left Jew Street in 1991. An elderly lady who lives on the street said the Jews were good neighbors and she misses her friends. There is no reason to doubt her sincerity.

Anti-Semitism
There was very little open anti-Semitism in Albania which, like most Communist states, made anti-Semitism illegal, but that doesn't mean there was a total absence of anti-Semitism. In the early 1950s, when there was the so-called "Doctors' Plot" to kill Stalin, the official policy against anti-Semitism was ignored by the hard line Communists who made strong anti-Semitic statements. Albania, in the early 1950s, was a Stalinist country and followed the lead of the Soviet Union. According to Jakoel, the anti-Semitism was by the Government and not the people.

Anti-Semitism, where it did exist, was more of the name calling variety then organized physical actions. One accusation was that there was discrimination in gaining entrance to the University, but Jakoel disagreed and pointed out that there was so many Jewish graduates that it was impossible to claim any discrimination.[2]

Trades and Professions
The Jews of the Third Wave (last half of the 19th century), were merchants and trades men. The group arriving in Israel in 1991 were mostly professionals.

Assimilation and Conversion
Because of the nature of the atheistic society there was no problem in losing Jews to assimilation. Everyone knew who the Jews were, or thought they did, but this was of no interest to the general population. Albanian Jews were assimilated without loss of their Jewish identity. Conversions in and out of Judaism were very rare in modern times, but there is evidence that historically, before the 20th century, there were wholesale conversions to Islam. It's logical to assume that many of the non-Jews who accompanied their families to Israel will convert to Judaism for sake of convenience.

Names
Before the atheistic period the Sephardic custom was followed of naming babies for living persons. The first son was named for the paternal grandfather and the second son was named for the maternal grandfather.

In the atheistic period names given to children must not identify them by religion. Some parents had given their children Biblical or Koran names, but in 1976 the Government ordered that these children must assume non-religious names.

Money to Buy Land in Israel
Jakoel told about the custom, before the World War, of contributing funds to buy land in Palestine. There was a little blue and white box with a Star of David on it, on the wall into which small coins were placed by the children every sabbath. The parents held the little children up so they could reach the box and deposit the coins which would be used for the liberation of the lost homeland. Once a year a representative of the fund came to empty the box. This practice was common among American and other Jews of the same generation.

Emigration From Albania Before 1991
When the war ended about half of the Jewish population left Albania for Israel, Yugoslavia and elsewhere. This left

approximately 300 Jews in Albania, a small number, but nearly double the number in the prewar period.

In 1949, many of the remaining Jews tried to emigrate to Israel, but the Government denied them exit visas. At that time Albania was a part of the Soviet Bloc which was anti-Zionist and opposed Jewish emigration as concessions to the Arab nations they were courting. Even after the break with the Soviets, Albania's dictator maintained an anti-Israel, anti-Zionist position which is hard to understand. The period up until the 1990s was the time of isolation and Albania didn't make exceptions for Moslem countries and they weren't courting the Arabs, yet the anti-Israel propaganda continued

Hoxha prohibited Jews from emigrating to Israel and took a strong anti-Israel position. Albania did not establish diplomatic relations with Israel until six years after his death.

Most anti-Zionist propaganda is anti-Semitic, but this wasn't the case in Albania. Anti-Israel propaganda was widely distributed, but at least on its face it wasn't anti-Semitic and it was not directed towards Albania's small Jewish population.

Footnotes:
1. March 13, 1953, p. 36.
2. At the time the University of Tirana had 8 faculties and 16,000 students. There were two Higher Education Institutes in Albania. Education at all levels is free. There have been additional higher education facilities.

Chapter Eleven

The Righteous Among the Nations

The State of Israel created a program to identify and honor non-Jews who risked their lives to rescue Jews during the Holocaust. More that 12,000 individuals have been honored so far. The granting of Righteous status is not taken lightly and there must be adequate proof to justify being honored. Unfortunately, many deserving persons will never be recognized for a myriad of reasons. In some cases, the Righteous was murdered by the same Germans who murdered the Jews. In some instances, the Jews died before being able to identify their would be rescuers. There was also a period of a lack of communication between Israel and the Soviet block countries, Poland and Albania to name two, which made it difficult to get the information and documentation needed to establish Righteous qualification.

When the Albanian Jews arrived in Israel they had not forgotten their Moslem and Christian friends who risked their lives to protect them from the ravages of the Holocaust. Josef Jakoel brought to Israel files he and other Jews had created to document the deeds of the Righteous. These files were created over a period of years, because he knew that someday he would be able to get these files to Israel so the Righteous would get the long overdue recognition they deserve. This resulted in seventeen Albanians being recognized as Righteous. There are other Righteous from Albania who were recognized by other documentation.

Being designated as Righteous entitles the individual to automatic honorary citizenship in the State of Israel, and in some instances financial assistance based on need. The financial assistance is provided by the New York based

Jewish Foundation for the Righteous, an independent organization of American and Canadian Jews committed to helping deserving and needy Righteous.

This was the only country under German occupation during the World War where Jews were not killed. The generosity and heroism of the Albanian people has not been adequately recorded and acknowledged.

Righteous Gentile Program
Israel created the Righteous Gentile program to honor those non-Jews who risked their lives to shelter Jews during the Holocaust years. The program is operated by Yad Vashem, an agency of the Israeli Government.

Each candidate for Righteous status is vetted to determine eligibility. Most Righteous are deemed eligible when Yad Vashem receives letters from two sponsors who attest to the fact that the gentiles being considered risked their lives. Most often it is the Jew who was sheltered by the Gentile being considered who initiated the process. A visit to Israel is not required for accreditation and most Righteous have never visited Israel.

Those Righteous who visit Israel can participate in a beautiful ceremony honoring them for their deeds of half a century ago. Until a few years ago, planting a tree in the Garden of the Righteous at Yad Vashem was a part of the ceremony. However, the expansion of Yad Vashem is not possible because of its hill top location and it's impossible to plant more trees. There just isn't any more room. In lieu of the tree planting, a series of walls have been created for bronze plaques to be affixed with the name of each Righteous and his country. The bronze plaques for the Albanian Righteous were among the first affixed to these walls.

Righteous Gentiles Visit Israel
In 1993, all Albanian Righteous Gentiles who had not yet been to Israel were invited to the Holyland as the guests of

Harvey Sarner, to be honored by the State of Israel and the Jewish people. Some of the invited Righteous had passed away and others were to sick or infirmed to make the trip. In a number of incidents the Righteous parent, who was physically able to make the trip, asked if a son or daughter could go in his or her place. The parent felt it was important that the child learn more about the world outside Albania. Following the wishes of the Righteous, about one third of the group visiting Israel were children or other relatives of the Righteous.

The 17 Righteous and relatives spent a week in Israel as my guests. In addition to participating in the beautiful ceremony at Yad Vashem, the guests had reunions with the Albanian Jews, most of whom were living in absorption centers learning Hebrew and getting acclimated to their new country. The demonstrated affection and emotion at the reunions was sincere. Watching the people hugging and kissing it was impossible to tell which were the Jews, Christians or Moslems.

The guests also visited sites holy to Jews, Moslems and Christians, learned about life in Israel and generally visited the usual tourist attractions.

Instead of giving them the usual souvenirs to take home they were given boxes of food to share with their families and friends. Happily, the famine in Albania has since come to an end.

Exodus 1991
In 1991 the Jews of Albania left their homeland. After a presence of two thousand years the Jewish community ceases to exist except for a handful of strays who couldn't bring themselves to leave friends and family. Most of the few remaining Jews are married to gentiles who were unwilling to emigrate.

The analogy between Josef Jakoel and Moses can't be avoided. It was like Moses leading the people of Israel out

of Egypt, but there is one major difference. Moses led the people from a land of bondage and oppression and there was no remorse at the departure. Jakoel led his people from a land they loved and away from life long friends.

A few identifiable Jews remained behind. These were mostly families with heavy intermarriage where it was decided that keeping the family together was of paramount importance. Two families returned to Albania. The pull of gentile family members left behind and the strangeness of the language and culture overwhelmed them. Perhaps they expected too much.

It is not an overstatement to credit Josef Jakoel and his daughter, Felicita, with responsibility for the Exodus and herein lies a story of great adventure. Someone had to make a secret trip to Israel. Josef would have been the logical one but his poor health made this impossible. Felicita was chosen. She had good health and the enthusiasm of youth.

In 1990, Felicita Jakoel obtained an exit visa to allow her to leave Albanian to visit distant relatives in Greece. After years of complete isolation, Albania was permitting its citizens to make limited excursions abroad. With the aid of the Israeli Ambassador to Greece, Felicita was able to proceed from Greece to Israel. This important step was not taken without some trepidation and fear. Felicita violated Albanian law when she proceeded to travel in excess of her exit visa, which was limited to travel in Greece. She had a definite fear of imprisonment upon her return to Albania. The fear was justified but it didn't deter her.

Once in Israel she contacted various organizations, including the Jewish agency, where the framework was established for the exodus of Albanian Jewry

In the offices of the Jewish Agency in Israel, Felicita produced a secret list of all the known Jews in Albania. Her visit to the Jewish Agency resulted in a coordinated

action with the Israeli and Italian Governments, and the American Joint Distribution Committee.

Felicita spent 12 days in Israel planning the exodus and planning her return to Greece, and then on to Albania. The Israeli Embassy in Athens made the arrangements for her return. Everything was done secretly, as there were no diplomatic relations between Israel and Albania at that time. Before returning she contacted her father who assured her that it was safe to return to Albania. The political climate had changed and Albania was opening its doors to permit limited emigration. Once she returned to Albania she still felt a need for secrecy as she couldn't be sure how the Albanian Government would react to what she had done

While Felicita was in Greece and Israel there were riots in Albania. Six thousand Albanians went into foreign embassies, sometimes forcing their way in. After much hesitation, and many discussions, the Albanian Government agreed to permit the emigration of these masses. It still was dangerous for Felicita to admit that she had been to Israel. The fading dictatorship was exercising its last powers and no one wanted to be sacrificed.

When Josef Jakoel received the good news from his daughter, he caused to be published an announcement in an Albanian newspaper entitled, "Nothing is to be forgotten" which described the wonderful attitude of the Albanian people towards the Jews during the Second World War. This was the first time the Government allowed such an article to be published. The article made a big impression bringing back many memories and causing endless discussion.

The Jews knew very little about Israel and most of what they knew came from the Communist press. For years the Albanian newspapers had used negative and insulting language when mentioning Israel. The only other source of information was Jakoel's translations of information, and

his distribution of books and articles about Israel. When Felicita returned, she brought with her a supply of books about emigration and the possibilities of going to live in Israel.

Jakoel couldn't advertise in an Albanian newspaper asking Jews considering emigrating to Israel to contact him. But the news asking Jews considering emigration to Israel to contact him was spread from mouth to mouth. The Jakoels were contacted by virtually every Jewish family from throughout the country, including some who they had not known to be Jews. Prior to the exodus, about half of the Jews were living in Tirana and half in Vlora. There were individual families in Shkodra, Fier, Lezha, and other small towns. Representatives of every Jewish family came to Tirana, to Jakoel's home, to talk about emigration.

There were a few "closet" Jews who visited Jakoel. After declaring themselves as Jews or as "part Jews" they wanted to talk about emigration. Jakoel expressed some cynicism about these "new Jews" who wanted to emigrate to Israel. They knew very little about Judaism. Their lack of familiarity with things Jewish was attributed to the anti-religious policies of the Government. Jakoel was suspicious that non-Jews were claiming to be Jews as a way of getting out of Albania.

In December, 1990, there were mass protests against the Government which resulted in the progressive collapse of the dictatorship in late January, and early February, 1991. The dictatorship was ending at exactly the time the first group of Jews emigrated to Israel. The first group arrived in Israel on the last day of the Gulf War, in January, 1991, with the majority arriving in May, 1991.

The political and economic conditions further deteriorated as free elections were held and the dictatorship ended. The new Albanian Government had no objections to the Jews emigrating to Israel, and diplomatic relations were established between the two countries The emigration was conducted in accordance with Albanian law.

The Jews were in an excellent position as they had a place to go[1] and financial support. The costs of the move to Israel were paid by various agencies of the Israeli Government, and by some Jewish organizations. At the same time there were 6,000 Albanians living outside the country as refugees looking for appropriate final destinations.

Jakoel estimated that at least 10% of those emigrating were not Jews, with the majority of the non-Jews being spouses of Jews. His estimate is probably on the low side.
According to a spokesman for the Jewish Agency, "spouses, children and grandchildren of Albanian Jews can claim Israeli citizenship and have the same rights as Jews."

The Albanian Jews who went to Israel came under the Israeli "Law of Return" which gives immediate Israeli citizenship to any Jew who wants to settle in Israel.

"I love Albania. It's my second home," was Jakoel's answer when asked about Albania. The overwhelming majority are "pro-Albania," but not all of the new Israelis share Jakoel's attitude and love for Albania. He felt this minority confused the difference between the Albanian people and the Albanian Government.

Like all emigrants the Albanians criticize Israel, e.g. the laws relating to marriage and divorce, but like all Israelis they love the fact that they can openly criticize their government without fear of retribution.

For the Jakoel family emigration was a life long dream. It's conjecture as to how many of the Albanian Jews shared Jakoel's unmitigated Zionism,[2] but he was not alone. At the reunion of the emigrants and the Righteous a proud grandfather paraded around the room showing his grandchild to everyone. The single word he spoke over and over again, spoke volumes, "Sabra, Sabra."[3] He had come home to Israel and the birth of his grandchild completed the homecoming.

1991 Emigration

Jews were not the only Albanian citizens who wanted to escape from famine and oppression in 1991. According to newspaper reports, more than 10,000 Albanians had converged on Vlora and other ports desperate to join an exodus by sea. The objective was Italy, but only a few thousands reached the Italian shores.

By the time the majority of would be emigrants arrived at Vlora and Durrës there were no ships in these ports. The ships and small boats had moved as a flotilla with near disastrous results. For example, 600 were rescued from a sinking fishing boat just off the coast of Durrës.

The Albanian Government declared its main ports military zones as a away of giving itself the appearance of legality in keeping the crowds away from the ports.

Reaching Italy wasn't the solution. In March, 1991, the Italian Government announced it was sending back to Albania more than 12,000 Albanian refugees who thought they had reached a sanctuary. Being denied sanctuary in Italy was contrasted to Jews being granted asylum in Albania.

The consequences of being sent back to Albania wasn't a horror on a par with the Holocaust, and there were much fewer numbers involved, but it was saddening to see a people being denied asylum when they had been so generous in granting it to others one generation earlier.
Famine was rampant in Albania in 1991, and two personal experiences made the problems known very quickly.

Upon his arrival in Israel, an Albanian asked which hour of the day would there be water. Never having to deal with the logistics of gathering enough water during one hour each day, it took more than a moment to appreciate the problem.

91

The other incident was full of pathos. Dining in one of Jerusalem's finer restaurants, an Albanian Righteous put down his knife and fork and said, "I can't eat this knowing how little my family is having for dinner tonight."

Conditions have improved in Albania. Water is still rationed and food is available, but Albania still has the unwanted distinction of being the poorest country in Europe.

The Jews of Albania were the fortunate few. They had an inspiring leader and outside assistance from an agency of the Israeli Government. It's remarkable that while it was denying the right to emigrate, to tens of thousands of its citizens, the Albanian Government allowed the Jews to leave.

The Jewish Exodus was in accordance with Albanian law, which was very important because it meant that the Jews could come back to Albania to visit family and friends without fear of being arrested. The 300 Jews were a small matter to the Albanian Government considering the size of the other emigration movements, but it wasn't a small matter for the Jews of Albania.

The Jewish Agency carefully planned the movement of 300 people to avoid publicity which might have caused the Government to terminate the emigration. The Albanians came through Italy and Greece in small family groups over the course of several months. The Exodus was intelligently arranged and administered.

Albania Today
The Israel-Albanian Friendship League was formed in 1993 with 300 Albanian members, and dedicated to improve relations between the two peoples. They requested that the Israeli Government send them educational materials to replace the anti-Israel propaganda materials that had been distributed over the country.

SHOQATA E MIQESISE
Shqiperi - Israel
TIRANE

ASSOCIATION D'AMITIE
Albanie Israel
TIRANA

Honourable Mr.Harvey,

in our last meeting,the chair of the friendship
association Albania-Israel discused the way You financed and the warm
welcome You offered the first albanian group made up of 16 persons who
visited Israel.

For more than 50 years, the last regime in Albania not only hindered
to keep in touch with our friends in Israel, but did its best to insult Your
country. Its a task of this association and many other of Israel in Albania,
to make Your known here. We must build the bridge of friendship between
our two peoples and make it stronger and stronger every day.

The group that have been there and saw with their own eyes, what a
hard-working and talented people can do, are doing well in this direction.

It is You that made the visit of the Albanian group possible, giving so
the oportunity that they could see not only the achievements of Israel
people, but to feel the friendship these people were offering us.

On this occasion, our chairmanship declare You, and it is very
honoured to do that, "Righteous President" of our association.

We wish that the friendship between our two peoples with the
sincerity it is characterized, keeps growing every day, so our two peoples
could feel like real brothers.

Wishing you heartly good health and long life, on the behalf of the
chairmanship and of the albanian group of 16 persons, we thank You and
send You our best regards, making You sure that you have a lot of friends
in Albania.

Your respected name will remaind forever in the history book of our
association.

For the chair of the friendship
association Albania-Israel

Secretary
Henrik Prendushi

President
Refik Veseli

93

The concert mentioned earlier in honor of the Righteous Gentiles was a wonderful step in improving cultural relations between Israel and Albania.[4] There's so much that can and will be done. There's now two way airline traffic between the two countries, with the Righteous Albanians visiting their Jewish friends and the Albanian Jews returning to visit relatives and old friends. The Albanian-Jewish emigrants are an important bridge between the two countries, may they both prosper.

There are some traps that hopefully can be avoided in the future. The missionary zeal in Albania is unprecedented and we must hope that religion can return to Albania (if it was ever gone) without destroying Albania's history of religious tolerance and good will among the various denominations. The war just over the border, in what once was Yugoslavia, must be checked at the border and not allowed to spill over into peaceful Albania.

1992 was the last year of the Communist dictatorship and the country has moved fast into the modern era, but it has a long way to go. Albania has no enemy and it's just a matter of time before Albania will take its rightful place among progressive nations.

Footnotes:
1. Not everyone elected to go to Israel, about 35 decided to emigrate to America. Jakoel attributed this to the fact that they had relatives living in the United States.
2. There are those who emigrated to improve quality of life or to escape an oppressive government. Giving their children a better chance of finding a Jewish spouse was the attraction for some. Living openly as a Jew was an incentive for others.
3. The Hebrew word for a cactus that is hard on the outside and soft on the inside, used to describe a native born Israeli.
4. Participating in the commemoration were the Kibbutz Orchestra of Israel, the National Choir of Albania and members of the Opera Orchestra of Tirana.

A Short (incomplete) Bibliography

Books:

Amery, Julian, Sons of the Eagle: A Study in Guerilla War, 1948, Macmillan, London.

Dalven, Rae, The Jews of Ioannina, 1990, Cadmus Press, Phila., PA.

Grunbaum, Irene, Escape Through the Balkans, 1996, University of Nebraska Press, Lincoln, NE.

Hoxha, Enver. The Anglo-American Threat to Albania: Memoirs of the National Liberation War, 1982, Tirana, "8 Nentori".

Kotani, Apostol, Albania and the Jews, 1996, Albania.

Marmullaku, Ramadan, Albania and the Albanians, 1975, Anchor Books, London.

Newbigin, Marion I., Geographical Aspects of Balkan Problems, 1915, Putnam, NY.

Sarner, Harvey, The Jews of Albania, 1992, Brunswick Press.

Shaw, Stanford J., The Jews of the Ottoman Empire and the Turkish Republic, 1991, NYU Press, NY.

Swallow, Charles, The Sick Man of Europe-Ottoman Empire to Turkish Republic 1789-1923. 1973, Ernest Benn Ltd, London.

"Symmachos" Greece Fights On, n/d, Lindsay Drummond, Ltd, London.

Vickers, Martha, The Albanians, 1995, I.B. Tauris, London & New York.

Encyclopedias:

Universal Jewish Encyclopedia, vol.12, p.157.

Encyclopedia Judaica, Vol.2 pp.522-3 (Albania);Vol.14 p p.231 (Romaniots).

Articles:

Albanian Life, Jews in Albania, Farrel, Patrick (1990); History of Jews in Albania and the Balkans.

Destani, D.B. (editor) The Albanian Question (1996), Albanian Community Centre, London.

Forward, Albanians Reach Holy Land Before
"Messiah", January 8, 1993, New York, p.1.
Gushee, David P., Why They Helped the Jews,
Christianity Today, Oct. 24, 1944, p.33-35.
Puto, Artan. Jews of Albania on the Eve of WW II,
October, 1996 (?); The Effort (In Albanian)
Schwartz, Stephen. A Note on 17th Century Albanian
Jewry. Albanian Catholic Bulletin, (1994) vol.XV,
p.154-156, San Francisco; Some Notes About Albanian
Jews, (1991) vol.XII; Albanians of all Religions in
Solidarity with Persecuted Jewish Minority, (1989)
vol.X.
Trix, Frances, The Resurfacing of Islam in Albania.
January 1995, East European Quarterly XXVIII, no.4,
p.533-547.
Young, Antonia, Deciphering The Code, Illyria, Feb.1,
1995, p.6.
New York Times, Joyful Jews from "Another Planet"
called Albania, April 11, 1991.
Jewish Chronicle, London: May, 29, 1891, p.7; Mar. 9,
1894, p.9; Jan. 29, 1909, p.8; Mar. 13, 1953, p.36; May
30, 1958, p.1; Aug. 11, 1967, p.14; Jun. 8, 1973, p.23.
Jewish Daily Bulletin: NY Vol.XI, no. 2821 p.1, April
17, 1934. Editorial Notes by Herman Bernstein,
continued April 18, p.1.
Liria: Harvey Sarner, A Most Unusual Man, October-
November, 1995, p.7; Tirana Concert Commemorates
heroic rescue of Jews by Albanians during Holocaust,
October-November, 1995, p.2.

Unpublished:
Letter and memoir from Johanna Jutta Neumann to Van
Christo, dated March 20, 1995, "A Tribute to the
Albanian People."
Josef Jakoel, Jews of Albania (in Italian).
British Government Documents.
PRO File FO 371/37138.
Albania Basic Handbook: Part 1, Pre-Invasion, March,
1943; Part 2, Post Invasion, Aug., 1943, "Secret".

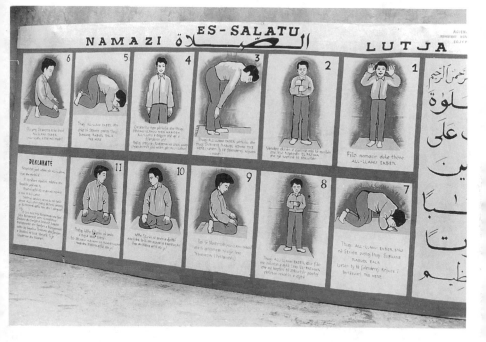

Instructions for Moslem prayer positions.

Mihal Lekatari and Shyqyri Myrto.

The Magen David was found in the old market of Elbasan,
which earlier had been called, "The Market of the Jews."

(L to R) Felicita Jakoel sitting with her father, Josef
and her mother.

Beqir Qoqja, a Righteous visiting Bethlehem.

(L to R) Mihal Lekatari and a member of the Jewish family from Yugoslavia, whom he rescued.

Josef Jakoel's sister, Eftihia Matalia, and her two children.
Raised in Albania, Eftihia married a Greek Jew and moved
to Corfu, Greece. They did not survive the Holocaust.

A large Jewish family in Ioannina, in 1943. Only the two young girls seated on the floor to the right survived the Holocaust. One survived by escaping into Albania.

BANKOVITSH FRED
BARKAN ANTON & HELENA
BINKEVICH-SIDIRAPULO VALENTINA
FIMBOYER ANA
GAEVSKAYA EMILIA
IGNATIEV PIOTR & VARVARA
KARCHEVSKAYA MARIA
KATENEVA OLGA
KELLER MARIA & SON ARNOLD
KLEBAIS MARGARETA & SISTER ALEKSANDRA
KRUMINS ARTURS & ERNA & DAUGHTER ILGA
METERS VELTA
MICKO VLADIMIR
MIELEIKE ELSA & MOTHER
MIKULOVA-AFANASIEV MINADORA
NOIM ANDRIANA
OZOLIN EDUARD & ANNA & SONS JANIS & VOLDEMAR
PETERSON MARTIN & MILDA
PETROVA YEFROSINIA & FEDOT
PILSROZE LINA
SEDUL ROBERT & JOHANNA
SKERSHKANE LEOKARDIA
SKUYINSH KATERINA
SPIRIDOVICH HELENA
STRELIS AMALIA
TROFIMOV SERGEI & VASA & DAUGHTER STEFANIDA
VANAGS KLARA & ANTON & DAUGHTER SKAIDRITE
VILMANS PETRUNELA
WARUSHKINA ULITA
ZVAIGZNE VILIS
ארמניה
ARMENIA
ՀԱՅԱՍՏԱՆ
TADSCHOJIAN ARAM & FELICIA
JERETZIAN ARA
HALAMLIEV SHAMAIL & FERDAUS & CHILDREN SULTAN & MUCHTAR
IVANOV PROKOP & LIDIA
JEMELINOVA JEVGENIA
KOLESNIKOVA YEKATERINA
KOROVIN SEMEN & KSENIA
MAXIMOVA VARVARA
אלבניה
ALBANIA
SHQIPËRI
BORICI SHAQIR & QAMILE & DAUGHTER BAHRIYA
BUDO SHYQYRI & XHEMILE
CIFTIA AGOSTIN & GYSEPINA & CHILDREN MARGERITA CESARINA & GJOVONA
DESTAN BALLA & LIMA
HOTI HASSAN & MOTHER FIFA & DAUGHTER CELJA & VEHBI
HOXHA NURO
HOXHA SHABAN & SIAVET & SON HILMI
KADIU BESIM & AISHE
KASAPI ZYRHA & SON HAMDI
KONA VASIL & KRISTINA
LEKATARI MIHAL
MECE SULEIMAN & ZENEPE
MUASIL DULAJ
MYRTO ABDULLA & TJE
MYRTO SHYQYRI
NOSI VASIL & KELKIRA & BROTHER NOSI & SISTER ADELINA
ORGOCKA PASKAL & LEFKOTHEA
QOQJA BEQIR
RULI METIN AZIZ & SHPRESA
SHEKO STAVRO & NORA
SHKURTI PIETRO & MAGDALENA
SHPUZA ESHREF
TOPTANI ATIF & GANIMET
VESELI VESEL & FATIMA & SON REFIK
XHYHERI QAMIL & HANUME

Standing before the wall listing the names of the Righteous is Johanna J. Neumann. (See page 58)

(L to R) Battino, Mrs. Mecaj, the author and Mr. Mecaj.